# ACQUIRING

# NEW

# ID

## How to Easily Use the Latest Computer Technology to Drop Out, Start Over, and Get On with Your Life

Ragnar Benson

PALADIN PRESS
BOULDER, COLORADO

.75

**Also by Ragnar Benson:**

Breath of the Dragon: Homebuilt Flamethrowers
Bull's Eye: Crossbows by Ragnar Benson
Do-It-Yourself Medicine
Eating Cheap
Gunrunning for Fun and Profit
Hard-Core Poaching
Home-Built Claymore Mines
Homemade C-4: A Recipe for Survival
Homemade Grenade Launchers
Live Off the Land in the City and Country
Mantrapping
Modern Weapons Caching
The Most Dangerous Game: Advanced
    Mantrapping Techniques

New and Improved C-4
Ragnar's Action Encyclopedia of Practical
    Knowledge and Proven Techniques
Ragnar's Action Encyclopedia Volume Two
Ragnar's Big Book of Homemade Weapons
Ragnar's Guide to Home and Recreational Use
    of High Explosives
Ragnar's Homemade Detonators
Ragnar's Ten Best Traps
Survival Poaching
Survivalist's Medicine Chest
The Survival Retreat
Switchblade: The Ace of Blades

*Acquiring New ID: How to Easily Use the Latest Computer*
    *Technology to Drop Out, Start Over, and Get On with Your Life*
by Ragnar Benson

Copyright © 1996 by Ragnar Benson
ISBN 0-87364-894-3
Printed in the United States of America

Published by Paladin Press, a division of
Paladin Enterprises, Inc., P.O. Box 1307,
Boulder, Colorado 80306, USA.
(303) 443-7250

Direct inquiries and/or orders to the above address.

# TABLE OF
# CONTENTS

# WARNING

Some of the techniques discussed in this book might be illegal in certain localities. Neither the author nor the publisher is advocating any illegal actions, nor is either responsible for the use or misuse of information contained herein. This information is *for academic study only*.

# PREFACE

At least 20 years have elapsed since the following incident occurred, so I can relate it without damaging anyone's reputation.

Two neat, well-groomed men stopped at a small-town chamber of commerce office. The pair were articulate, and in their $600 suits they exuded a presence not usually found among the information-seeking *hoi polloi* who came through the door. The female receptionist thought the pair quite striking in their beefy way. Others in the grungy office reckoned the two to be stereotypical well-appointed, well-conditioned retired U.S. Marine Corps officers.

The duo stated their mission to be gathering whatever information they could on two specific local businesses and their small-town proprietors, the county's only undertaker and a prominent "good-ol'-boy" country attorney. Both local residents were respected and successful—proverbial pillars of the community.

The strangers pelted the chamber of commerce employees with questions about the undertaker and the attorney. How long had they been in business? Who were their clients? Could someone describe their volume, market share, physical plants, and equipment? The outsiders were not pushy or tough; they asked their questions tactfully, and listened politely to the responses, but basically the observers felt that any offered information was immediately snapped up, cataloged, and stored for easy retrieval.

Meanwhile, the owner of the local credit bureau/collection agency wandered into the office to pick up a city map for a visiting relative. The minute this fellow—now long gone to his reward—saw the two strangers, he blanched and turned around to leave before his presence was noted. His retreat was blocked by arriving "two-weeks-with-pay" types. All he could do was scurry over to the corner wall, where he intently scrutinized the office charter, a document no one had read in years, hoping desperately that he remained unseen.

Presently the pair walked back out to their black Caddy, unlocked the doors (another thing that set them apart; most people in the small town never even locked their houses), and drove off toward the offices of the two city fathers. Only after the strangers' departure did the credit bureau man turn from the wall.

"Let's go into your back office," he almost pleaded to the director of the chamber. As soon as the door slammed, he blurted out in terror: "Those fellows are free-lance professional bill collectors. They travel around this four-state area collecting sour gambling debts. Since no laws apply, they follow no rules and regulations. Their only rule is to get the money."

It was horrifyingly apparent that our town undertaker and attorney spent too much time in Las Vegas, and it wasn't spent watching the dancing girls. No one had thought to look at the Caddy's license plates, but it was assumed that the two strangers had come directly from Las Vegas.

I vividly recall that the undertaker and attorney kept low profiles for the next several months after their encounter with the two enforcers, who eventually roared back. But we never learned what actually transpired. My guess is that even the gamblers' wives didn't know.

* * *

Although the idea later became popular, this was the first time I contemplated the concept of dropping out and assuming a new identity. Depending on the severity of their offense, I began to reason, these two guys really could have profited by knowing how to disappear. Of course, there was a great deal more to it than hiding in their lake cabins for a couple of weeks, but it was interesting to plot various courses of action they could have taken, especially if the alternative was two broken legs.

It seemed painfully obvious that there were situations when even city fathers might want to know how to quickly and easily disappear—over and above the obvious legal, criminal, and domestic crunches that usually force people underground.

Some of us have given a lot of thought and study to these problems and how we might put together a plan to deal with them. Seems as though having some sort of system thought out and in place, ready to go when needed, is part of life in our modern society.

Who can predict when love might turn to hate or a comfortable income might reverse into bankruptcy? Obscure, unpredictable rules and regulations confront businessmen and could rear up and ensnare any of them. Currently, many small businessmen, for instance, find themselves at the mercy of illogical, unpredictable, often foolish environmental, social, and liability laws. At a time when prisons should be full of criminals, we find honest property owners who are fugitives as a result of having cut down a tree, been falsely accused by a former employee of harassment or discrimination, gotten rid of pests on their land or in their houses, or improperly dumped a load of dirt on their property. Simply using one's building for activities not approved by a local planning and zoning commission can, these days, lead to a long stay in the "Gray Stone Hotel."

The necessity of efficiently and officially disappearing has become dramatically more important. At the same time a very real dilemma exists: as a practical matter, those with enough money and smarts to orchestrate their disappearance usually cannot do so because closing existing businesses cuts off needed cash flow, and moving away to start over is never feasible if the plan is to start another identical business. Investigators, both private and public, will pierce that veil instantly.

This has been the Gordian knot facing people in search of new identities. Traditional new-identity instructions mostly failed to appreciate this dilemma. Modern, high-tech developments have dramatically changed the new identity business, but either by design or purpose, no one is talking about the financial element.

Most of the information out there was gathered 15 years ago and is either much too difficult to implement or is impractical, given modern computers. It also does not reflect the truth that government agencies do not like people who assume new identities and have changed the ground rules dramatically.

Of course, what follow is *for academic study only*. As one attorney told me while being interviewed for this book, "If for some reason the government wants to pick you up and lock you away, there is always a law that will allow it to do so. There is absolutely *no* way the average citizen—which we all are—can live a perfectly legal life any more."

It is both easier and more essential to know how to disappear successfully than it ever has been. To that end this book is dedicated.

# INTRODUCTION

Beginners at this business of establishing a new identity should take careful note of the history of their endeavor. As the old saw goes, those who cannot remember the past are condemned to repeat it.

Informed people often differ in their interpretation of events, but some agreement exists suggesting that the art and practice of new-identification acquisition first evolved 15 years ago in response to needs of 1960s counterculture people. These folks often had bad academic records or criminal charges and owed large sums of money for school debts and foolish judgments they allowed themselves to be drawn into. Some had

1

Woodstock-generated marriages that never made sense.

More important, these citizens increasingly realized that the government, with which they were so intricately involved and on which they relied, did not have solutions to their problems. Many began to see government as a fearsome monster rather than a dutiful servant. Reacting with suspicion, they wanted out. "Let's start over" became the plaintive cry heard throughout the land. Most were basically very decent people, but they had a great deal to "start over from."

Study of the three aspects of new identity became common, as exemplified by such books on the subject as *Paper Trip I and II* by Barry Reid, *New I.D. in America* by Anonymous, and several others of less practicality and scope. Most of the new IDers who have actually "been reborn" claim that, as a practical matter, these books were unhelpful. Various reasons for this evaluation have been given. Most relate to the broad-brush approach that the books tend to take, which paints all situations similarly, and the fact that the information in this field—as in many others—quickly becomes dated.

Basically, these volumes analyze the three basic components of new ID, including false ID, counterfeit ID, and government-issued genuine ID that users carry and use but that was issued for someone other than them.

False IDs include the superficially official-looking photographer's, reporter's, pilot's, and private in-vestigator's badges or passes printed and widely sold by specialty mail-order houses that advertise in *Soldier of Fortune, U.S.A. Today*, and many other publications. You can purchase these showy, sturdy cards for about $5. Type in the pertinent information of your choosing, insert a color picture, laminate, and—lo and behold—you have an impressive-looking, but totally bogus card, claiming that the holder is an expert at nude photography, mercenary warfare, bodyguarding, or whatever. There are scores of different cards from which to choose.

These cards are lots of fun and sometimes effective

when mixed with other IDs. They are classed as third-level ID documents, which means they are fairly worthless when subjected to close inspection (more about the three levels of ID in Chapter 5). Yet they can be valuable to establish an employment history that will otherwise be completely lacking for anyone who is making a fresh start.

A second set of new ID includes those that closely mimic legal levels one and two real IDs (we'll discuss the three levels of ID in Chapter 5). Examples of these are credit cards, driver's licenses, passports, birth certificates, and other papers we use to establish who we are. We rely on them daily even though they became the bases for establishing ourselves years ago. Like false level-three ID cards, these documents will not hold up to close investigative scrutiny. They are the well-done forgeries that take advantage of modern electronic technology. These documents get exposed by experts, *not* by casual observers. Bank tellers, for instance, have no practical method of verifying a good counterfeit driver's license, although a cop on a routine traffic stop could easily do so by calling the dispatcher or running it through a computer housed in his vehicle, which is becoming more common.

If the truth be known, every personal ID, whether it is an excellent reproduction or someone else's valid document, can be detected by the right person or under the right circumstances. A good private investigator of my acquaintance brags, for instance, that he can find anyone, anyplace if you are willing to pay the bill. Using someone else's real birth certificate as a "breeder" document to generate new ID won't slow him a bit.

The important point concerning these computer-forged documents is that users must have a large, easily produced supply so that authorities can be continually fended off by additional sets of documents. Current field experience suggests that these forgeries can be used for a surprising length of time in more situations than one would initially suppose. For instance, Claude A. Dallas, wanted in Idaho for prison escape after being convicted of murdering a game warden, used a bogus library card, while on the run, to evade an immigration service roadblock.

The problem with these documents, on which authorities rely and which new IDers absolutely must have, is that it is highly illegal to sell blank, preprinted Social Security cards, driver's licenses, state birth certificates, or medical clinic billing forms. New ID mechanics recognize that several of these, done in appropriately matched names, could and would keep authorities at bay for a long time if you could obtain the forms. However, they offer no realistic suggestions as to how to secretly acquire the necessary master documents. Vague allusions are sometimes made to suppliers who have them, but these never contain any real information.

"Sweet-talk your local printer into running the blanks for you," one writer suggested, in all seriousness. Yeah, as if a printer is going to crank out short runs of blank Social Security, birth, or death certificates; pilot's licenses; or three-color Florida driver's licenses! Then tell me he will not either charge usurious prices, call the cops, or do hopelessly sloppy work. In any event, the printer will *always* spill his guts to the first investigator who shows up. Many complex criminal cases have been broken by investigators who took the time to canvass every printer in the region asking about nothing more than simple business cards.

A fourth set of documents that can be classified as levels one through three is much tougher to characterize accurately in just a few catchy words: the supposed originals that even skilled investigators cannot usually uncover. Admittedly, these documents are quite good, but they are also very difficult to assemble and they are *not* perfect. It takes time and energy, but good investigators can uncover these as well.

In this case, an example is probably better than a lengthy explanation. Securing a real birth certificate issued to a deceased person is the most common. Traditionally, someone desiring a new ID will look around for a child of the same sex and race as he or she, and who was born at about the same time but who died at from one to five years of age. Using that long-deceased kid's name, the prospective new IDer applies for a certified copy of the child's birth certificate from the county in which the kid was born. The county of birth must be different from the county of death, or the likelihood of being caught is inordinately large. Using this real document, new IDers can acquire Social Security cards, driver's licenses, and even valid passports.

However, this commonly suggested method is not foolproof. You have to invest a lot of time and energy to come up with the ideal candidate, and then you have to convince the county to send a copy of the birth certificate. Unlike even a few years ago, most counties now require a great deal more documentation before sending out birth certificates, including photocopies of supporting identity documents or notarized statements attesting to the requester's identity. Several people who have successfully changed identities and who are willing to talk about their experiences claim that the situation is much more complex now and becoming increasingly more so each day. Some counties are routinely cross-referencing their files against Social Security records and death certificates, although we are still far from a national system!

Ironically, the very complexity of the maze of electronic data bases designed to keep tabs on people that makes securing new-identity documents so much tougher can have the opposite effect. The truth is that government has become so overwhelming that, happily, the right hand often does not know what the left hand doeth. Convoluted bureaucratic rules and edicts are in place that, if accurately and completely collected and used against us, would essentially preclude any commerce. Fortunately for those looking to drop out and begin anew, either the various agencies haven't gotten together and exchanged information, their bureaucrats don't know how to implement the system, or they simply choose not to implement the rules. In one recent instance, a new IDer was allowed an extra year of grace simply because a sheriff's deputy didn't think current child-support payment regulations were fair. He didn't know the fellow's whereabouts, but he also refused to trigger data searches that might have uncovered him hiding under a new identity.

Another excellent example involves the Internal Revenue Service (IRS), which only recently started entering data on state vehicle registrations and bank account activity to correlate with individual tax filings. At great expense, the IRS procured massive computers and sophisticated software to achieve this. The Achilles' heel of the effort was that the IRS hardware and software were eight years old by the time they were up and running. Eight years equates to hopeless obsolescence in the world of computers. Absolute chaos characterized the entire IRS effort. Insiders claim that the IRS still doesn't know why the new automated system failed to work as promised.

So while new IDers must plan to minimize their exposure to cross-correlation, at the same time they should be prepared to use whatever confusion that they can orchestrate or hide behind to their own advantage. I have offered to bet the price of this book that only random telephone calls to the recorder's offices in various county seats in Indiana, Ohio, Illinois, and Kentucky will uncover the fact that all vital records have been lost to fire, flood, or stupidity some time within the last 50 years. My bet is that this pleasant fact will be uncovered before even 10 courthouses are surveyed. New ID mechanics who uncover these anomalies and can also turn up reasonable facsimile forms can use this records loss to their advantage. For example, I have in my possession a 1932 certified birth certificate that was done before a flood and can't be proven a forgery because the originals are all lost and it isn't even known for sure what format these documents took back then.

People who successfully work these systems must

be opportunistic, and they must be flexible. In my case, hospital records done at a small rural hospital were lost or accidentally destroyed during a remodeling project undertaken in the 1930s. Though authorities may be mildly suspicious of forged ID done at the hospital at the exact time of the remodeling, they probably won't be able to prove forgery immediately. They might not even try if enough convincing supporting documents are offered.

Our second great leap in new ID capability is the home manufacture of identity documents because of the dramatic advances in computer technology, especially in the realm of decreasing prices, increasing reliability, and user-friendly software. Flatbed color scanners, for instance, that sold for $1,800 two years ago now sell for $500, including necessary, very user-friendly software that alone cost about $1,000 till as recently as January 1996.

I have just purchased a new seven-pound computer with more and faster memory than the old vacuum tube-type machines my uncle used during the late 1950s and early 1960s. (His computer took up a whole floor of his office building!) Detailed chapters follow, but suffice it to say at this point that those in need can easily expect to purchase a computer for $1,500, a scanner, including software for $500, and a process color printer for $400. These printers will make credible $2 bills on high-rag bond paper!

One of the most immediate necessities for those seeking new IDs are authentic-looking business cards. These can be purchased at reasonable prices (about $45 per thousand), but who needs 1,000 similar business cards? Additionally, the printer may remember you should the authorities come asking.

It is far better to whomp out a series of two-color business cards, which will never be questioned, in the privacy of your home or office. You can use desktop publishing and a printer that will take card stock you have purchased discreetly from a distant stationery shop. I have even seen these homemade cards fool a U.S. Customs agent at the Canadian border.

Incredibly, current new ID mechanics report that the U.S. tax structure makes it easier than ever to disappear while still supporting oneself. All this has to do with the fact that taxes in general have increased to the point where they are so broad and confiscatory that it pays better to work in the underground barter, black, or tax-avoidance economy. In most places, working the black economy has become so common that no one thinks twice about it. A friend's cleaning lady recently told him that she was getting a divorce and needed more money, but that she would continue to work at the old rate if he paid cash. My friend wasn't planning to work in government or run for office, so he immediately snapped up the offer.

New IDers who must work outside the system without Social Security numbers, annual tax filings, quarterly reports, and the like can easily do so. They join the tens of thousands of Americans already working that way and arouse no special suspicion.

Publications as prestigious as the *Wall Street Journal* frequently carry in-depth features about people who work in the so-called black economy because they are precluded by race, formal training, local politics, finances, or whatever from acquiring needed permits and licenses. In many other cases, users of these various services cannot afford the high rates charged by those who are legally licensed and bonded who do work within the system; this establishes a demand for those who wish to supply goods or services under the table. It's a very Third World-like phenomenon that has increased exponentially in our country in just the past few years, providing yet another example of why it is relatively easy to make a living as a new IDer.

Newcomers, as well as old hands at this business, should realize that being a successful new IDer has changed and that a few innovative concepts have recently surfaced that make disappearing much easier than it was a few short years ago. The admonition for the wise is not to forget what worked a few years ago, but to realize that our society and, more important, our technology are rapidly changing.

# 1

# PLANNING IS THE TOUGH PART; EVERYTHING ELSE IS DETAILS

People who have successfully changed their ID are generally reluctant to talk about the methods they used. So it comes as no great surprise that, even though we may suspect that there are a number of successful new IDers out there, they are hard to find. However, given a modest amount of diligence, I was able to turn up a few who had successfully done it for the long term.

If these folks finally do talk, of course, they never give their last names—real or assumed. Floyd is one such example. He fled what he felt was an arbitrary and unfair court judgment in favor of his ex-wife. His plan, which he successfully implemented, was to drop out for as long as it took to get her to agree to a fair settlement.

"Settling the paramount issues necessary before becoming a new IDer is incredibly difficult," Floyd says, "even though they initially seem simple and straightforward. Successful new IDers must have these somewhat philosophical considerations firmly reasoned or their project is just so much fantasizing."

Whether it's because of an unhappy marriage, insurmountable debts, bad credit, an autocratic family, a criminal record, ties to family members who are socially unacceptable, an entanglement with dangerous gangster types, or whatever, a decision to start over should not be taken lightly. Those who don't plan adequately will waste a lot of time and money being unsuccessful: the brass ring comes only to those who think things through thoroughly.

Of his decision to disappear Floyd recalls, "I didn't know if it was going to be a year or whatever, but I did know that I was going to come back someday when things worked themselves out."

Floyd's problems were exacerbated by the fact that his imbroglio with his ex caught the attention of the IRS. Not only did he have to contend with a spiteful ex-wife, he also had minions of the IRS breathing down his neck. Yet Floyd still believes his project was a bit simpler than that of most new IDers, all things considered. Because he did intend to return, he kept most of his original identity, but in a new place.

Others with experience disagree, suggesting that it is tougher to retain your real identity in a new hiding place than it is to take on a completely new identity. Each person must decide before he sets out which plan is best suited to his needs.

Circumstances and situations change rapidly. Not only must a person decide that he is leaving for a new life, he must also seriously evaluate whether he will ever want to return. There are the matters of aging parents, spousal reform, the likelihood of a substantial inheritance, and the fact that police may actually catch the guy who really committed the crime—all of which may alter the person's desire to remain in a strange place without family or friends forever. In cases of serious criminal infractions, such as the ax murder of seven children, or especially effective offenses against key politicos or heavy hitters in the criminal community, it may not be possible to come back once a break is made. Some nasty federal authorities with unlimited budgets will tap a suspect's family phone, sort through his mail, and employ sound and video monitors on his premises until they finally develop the necessary leads.

Starting fresh after a breakout from the penitentiary, one has little chance to lay back money and supplies or decide on the best alternative plans of departure. But the point is that if new IDers wait too long to make a break, and then do it half-heartedly and not on a level commensurate with the dedication of those looking for them, the effort will fail.

A second point made by Floyd is also valid: new IDers not associated with a heinous crime or nefarious people do not need to execute their plan to the level of their more sought-after brothers in order to stay perfectly hidden. In other words, simple measures done in great profusion are just as effective in many circumstances as deep measures that are tough to implement.

Briefly, to successfully assume a new ID you must do the following:

- Make a firm, irrevocable decision to make the break, including setting a date for departure.
- To the best of your ability, decide whether it is conceivable that you may eventually wish to come back as your old self. Life is full of surprises, and things change dramatically. Some of the methods outlined in this book are practically irrevocable,

unless you are willing to encounter serious consequences.

Accurately and cold-bloodedly decide your personal threat level so that you can assemble a valid, workable plan. If you have bragged to others about your plan, successful execution is unlikely. It may still be essential to leave to become a new person, but if others know about even small portions of the plan, long-term success is extremely difficult to impossible, given current cash rewards for information.

In the case of people escaping just a hop ahead of some major ugliness, the first 60 days are, by a factor of 10, the most critical. In some cases it's the first 10 hours or even minutes if your planning or timing is really bad. Two separate but related issues concerning your first move in an emergency are (1) where to go till pursuing spouses, creditor, or minor minions of the law run out of time and money or lose most of their initial ardor, and (2) how to get there.

Getting there, according to some recent revelations on the part of our national police, is far more important than we may have first realized. "Before taking a journey, one must know the destination," goes an old Arab proverb. The advice about choosing a destination that I received from those who have done it was surprising and, to some extent, contradicted what older IDers espoused.

"Go far enough not to be recognized, to a place large enough to blend in, a destination that is not necessarily directly away from the point of danger," the newest IDers advise. This is also a general philosophy of the federal Witness Protection Program. In two cases I have looked at, this included heading to a small city in the general direction of the threatening ex-wife and an irate former business partner. These two erroneously assumed the man they wanted had gone farther west to disappear in a big city, rather than toward them to a dumpy little town.

A temporary residence can be taken in a cheap motel, work camp, or other unlikely flophouse where real names and identification are not required. One plucky fellow got a job in a small resort as a cook. He stayed there three weeks until he got his full plan together.

Crossing into Mexico or Canada may be an excellent strategy. In the case of a high-publicity criminal case or civil lawsuit, expect that the border guards will have been alerted. But under most circumstances, especially after a few days, guards on the Mexican or Canadian borders should not be a problem. Tens of thousands of workers, tourists, and family members cross these borders daily. The United States is not some banana republic—borders cannot be closed. Scrutiny for a single person of your description may be increased, and border guards may watch diligently for your vehicle. But among the tens of thousands crossing, this may be a minor threat.

In numerous cases, new IDers have elected to go to Canada or Mexico for the first 30 to 60 days till things cooled down and they weren't being sought with such vigor. Both Canada and Mexico require only a current photo driver's license to cross their borders. It has even been done with an international driver's license, which anyone can forge using the simplest of tools. If someone drives you in, not even a driver's license is required to get into Canada. U.S. border police just wave you by, and Canadian border police simply wave and smile in hopes that you are bringing lots of money.

Mexican border police require a current driver's license or certified copy of a birth certificate. Either one can be a forgery since these people are neither interested nor qualified in judging their authenticity. Taking a vehicle into Mexico is a hassle and not recommended because it leaves too much of a paper trail. Simply walk past the Americans and fill out an entry form for the Mexicans; the form is returned when you depart.

In either case it's an ideal point at which to trot out a

fake, computer-generated Florida driver's license or stamped, certified birth certificate. If travel is done by commercial carrier, these documents must be displayed when tickets are purchased in the United States. Ideally, you would use one set to leave town, going to an intermediate area still in this country, and then use a second driver's license and birth certificate to go from there across the border.

Problems usually arise trying to come back to the States, not going out. Inspections at the stations for U.S. citizens going across Canadian or Mexican borders are generally very cursory. This is a perfect example of the ease with which excellent computer-generated fake documents can be used with people who are really not able to verify authenticity instantly.

Choosing whether to flee to Mexico or Canada should not be based on geographical location alone. Canada is more civilized, organized, and expensive than Mexico; most Canadians speak English; and our northern border is extremely porous. Should new IDers not have time to put forged documents together, it is still relatively easy to slip into and out of Canada as necessary. At most, a two-mile walk through the timber is involved, and not even a fake ID is required. Since no records are kept, returning to the States even with an easy-to-produce international driver's license is easy. A close friend experimented a bit and had no problem.

Mexico is much more disorganized and, of course, Spanish speaking. But living is cheap and easy. Undocumented crossing into Mexico is possible but infinitely tougher than going into Canada. Even though you are much more likely to be stopped coming back into the States, your odds of sneaking back in with fake ID are still good. Because of hordes of people passing through ports of entry, U.S. border guards presently give driver's licenses and certified birth certificates only a cursory inspection.

Those on a limited budget who need a bit of space

can hang out on the cheap in Mexico while unobtrusively staying at one of the many resort communities. In some cases, short-time employment is possible as a carpenter, cook, computer operator or programmer, bookkeeper, or even a tout. You won't save money, but you should cover your living expenses. I know an American in Los Mochis who got a job as a spray plane pilot, which I always figured was tricky.

In any case, you will probably want to come back to the United States to establish a permanent new ID. Securing the documents needed to produce excellent forgeries while in a foreign country is next to impossible unless you have salted away a huge cache of cash. Even then, you may be nabbed going back to the salt mine for a resupply. One new IDer ran into a hapless refugee in Mexico who had a large, seemingly adequate supply of cash till the local police got wise. They didn't throw him out, because no reward in the States was offered; they just bled him white with requests for bribes. Finally, the undocumented fellow had to risk the river and return.

Keep in mind that all travel must be done under an alias. If possible, avoid credit cards, calls home to mother, purchase of oddball prescription drugs, and references to your past or any place or event that may indicate you are not who and what you say you are.

Universally, both new IDers and the police agree that most of the risk comes while driving to your destination. Charles Bahn, a professor of psychology and law, says, "People who are up to nefarious things often consider it inconsistent to obey traffic laws." Floyd, our benchmark successful new IDer, recognized that the greatest danger he faced until he could acquire a new driver's license was from traffic police. He had to worry about everything from being pulled over for having a burned-out taillight to having his driver's license recognized. "No license is better than a phony license that police can verify," he says. "Of course, I couldn't use my real license. I almost gave up and took a plane, but I needed the money I had in the car. It was one of the few big-ticket items I had that was paid off," he concludes.

California State Police officer Lt. Ron Casey claims that people involved in something illicit make police officers' jobs easier by driving too fast, too slowly, or erratically. Many law enforcement people report that random stops for minor traffic infractions result in more drug busts than the efforts of their entire antidrug units.

The message for new IDers who must depart by car or motorcycle is to drive very conservatively. Not too slow or fast, but very middle-of-the-road. Forged driver's licenses can be very useful, but not with a cop who pulls you over for a loud muffler.

Some new IDers recommend selling your vehicle and departing on public transportation. The problems are that you make yourself more traceable by this method, and it is virtually impossible to take along items that may be essential in your new role.

The best plan seems to be the following:

1. Loading your vehicle with essential clothes, computers, and cash.
2. Driving to an innocuous, small community.
3. Renting storage in a new name to store all goods but the essential personal items.
4. Driving your car to another city near the border and selling it.
5. Taking a bus to the border and walking across. Or you could purchase another cheap vehicle for cash and drive it across the border.

This plan won't succeed without cash, but as a practical matter, few new-ID programs will. Even becoming a street person who "will work for food" won't work without some start-up money. I'll get into how much money you'll need and how to budget it in Chapter 2.

# 2

# SUCCESS COMES TO THOSE WHO PLAN

Current new IDers all stress that anyone who leaves in a rush during the middle of the night, without money or planning, but with the hounds in hot pursuit, has little chance of success.

There is also a surprisingly broad consensus that, if a person was a total screw-up in his former life, he will probably behave in a similar way in his new identity. Police count on a bad actor's inability to change his ways as a means of preventing most people from becoming successful new IDers.

Financial planning should realistically assess the level of threat to be overcome and the extent to which you must go to overcome that threat, as outlined in the previous chapter.

Ken, who sells books and works on motorcycle to support himself, has planned his new life-style to be very frugal. This is in sharp contrast to his former life when he lived relatively high on the hog as a computer systems analyst. Ken's current financial plan is to live for a year on $300 per week, including room and board and vehicle expenses. He does not plan to work or have any other outside income, but as he points out, "an able-bodied person of average intelligence almost cannot escape finding work in our culture and economy." His surprising findings make up a great deal of the information in the chapter on working while under a new ID.

Ken's one-year budget is a minimum of about $20,000, which, because of the nature of his being in hiding, has to be cash. He also included $3,000 for purchase of new computer hardware and software and $500 for postage and supplies. This breaks out as follows:

| | |
|---|---|
| Weekly expenses @ $300 | $15,600 |
| Computer | $3,000 |
| Postage, paper, and supplies for documents | $500 |
| Miscellaneous expenses (or to purchase a used vehicle) | $900 |

All this has to be cash because authorities will quickly trace credit card and check transactions. Given the modern electronic strips imbedded in our currency, that amount of cabbage will set off a magnetic airport X-ray scanner, risking the threat of immediate confiscation, and you certainly would not check luggage containing cash. Whether at the hands of local police, airport security guards, the DEA, FBI, or whomever, that amount of long green—if discovered—will be confiscated. Deemed prima facie evidence of illicit activity, the hoard can be confiscated summarily by law enforcement agencies for their own use, without recourse on the part of the owner. This provides a great incentive for officials to uncover a citizen's cash cache.

An aspiring new IDer could find himself compromised at the very outset of his program. Bad luck, it is often said, doesn't usually happen by accident. Risks are avoidable or manageable if you plan for them.

Private and government investigators say that it is infinitely more difficult for two people to disappear together. Their common description is unique and fairly easy to track. Investigators can almost always find couples with kids by tracking the kids' school records. Our modern educational system won't permit kids to change schools without "their files." New schools won't admit the kids, and old schools call the authorities if the kids leave without orders to forward their files. One couple who disappeared for a couple of years went to Mexico so that they could put their kids in school there for about five months. They figured this was the only way they could succeed in dropping out. Of course, you could home-school for a couple of years, but this sometimes draws attention from just the sort of nosy government bureaucrats or busybodies you are hoping to avoid.

Escapees can minimize their cash outflow to some extent by working, but this is not the subject of this chapter. All new IDers recommend providing for the first year's living expenses without counting on any additional income.

Other than soup kitchens or panhandling, new IDers cannot accept public assistance of any kind. Numerous cases on record attest that people often use new identities to scam the welfare office. It certainly can be done, and has been done, but remember what you are trying to accomplish: to disappear. It seems unwise to add another layer of investigators who might blow your cover. Welfare workers say in private that it is relatively easy to get more than one helping of food stamps and welfare checks by becoming several different people, but that hundreds are caught each year in the process.

Public assistance offices require at least one photo ID, preferably a driver's license, and two supporting documents. Supporting documents can be a simple as library or club membership cards. Most bureaucrats know that their jobs depend on the number of clients they have and that raises are not generally given for filtering out fraud. Nevertheless, it is not recommended for people on the run.

Public assistance recipients are required to supply a Social Security number that is entered in a computer interfaced with the IRS, Department of Transportation, and the Social Security Administration. Social Security numbers are collated with current car ownership, income data, and other personal data to be doubly sure the application is plausible. It would appear to be safer and easier to produce food stamps with a desktop publishing system as opposed to applying for them using a false ID.

Nevertheless it will take money to start over. Not planning for this economic reality is unrealistic. Some places are pricier than others. On the theory that the best place to hide a tree is in the forest, large cities such as New York, Miami, or Seattle are good places to seek refuge. Going on the opposite theory that remoteness is best, it's north to Alaska. For different reasons, both kinds of places are expensive, difficult, and plagued by social disadvantages.

The admonition is to plan where to go based on the funds available. If a basic flophouse with enough privacy to start a document collection costs more than $200 per week at your intended location, then obviously a $20,000 per year budget won't cut it.

In the late 1970s, Jerry wanted to leave Boise, Idaho. He held several business and political positions of great importance, but he had an unpleasant marriage. He thought it would be fine as frog hair to move to a South Seas island. Jerry totted up the cost and, sure enough, he had sufficient funds, and that's where he probably went.

He planned so well that he left few tangible assets to keep the old home fires burning, which was certainly an important part of his plan since his ex didn't even have enough money to orchestrate a credible search.

Don't make the mistakes of calling or writing local chambers of commerce, travel agents, newspapers, or telephone companies for information at your target location and, most important, of talking to any friends about a possible retreat area, especially within six months of departure. Plenty of books are available in the library or bookstore. Investigators routinely check library and video checkout records, so don't check out any books about your planned location. If you intend to go to Mexico, leave behind books on Florida, Puerto Rico, or Washington state.

All telephone records can and will be seized through appropriate channels. Ex-spouses will recall correspondence, as will close friends when the reward gets high enough.

The advent of franchised fast-food restaurants makes the business of checking on local costs of living a bit simpler. Prices at McDonald's, Burger King, and Wendy's fluctuate somewhat by location, relative to the general cost of living. Using a pay phone, call the McDonald's in the city you have in mind. Their price of a standard Big Mac compared to that in your area will tell you volumes about the cost of living in the new place.

The quality of life in your new location would certainly suffer if you had to eat three meals a day at McDonald's for a full year, but you can easily calculate a food budget based on local McDonald's fare. Ken, the former computer analyst and active new IDer we discussed earlier, says that on a yearly basis, sticking mostly to small cities and including gas for his motorcycle, about $15 per day or $100 per week for food and fuel is about right. Not much room for many wine-and-candlelight meals in fancy restaurants, but this budget will get you out of Dodge in a pinch.

Clothes for your new life are not nearly as expensive as you might suppose. Dressing patterns must reflect local customs and be very inconspicuous. Mimi, another past participant in this process, claims she spent about $40 per year for adequate, warm clothing by shopping at yard sales, Goodwill, St. Vincent de Paul, Salvation Army, and any other inexpensive used-clothing stores. She is no fashion plate, but she is always sufficiently well dressed so as not to attract attention. The biggest problem, she says, is finding inexpensive shoes, which wear out more frequently than virtually any other item of clothing.

With greatly diminished responsibilities, those escaping will find their overhead for telephone, insurance, taxes, utilities, repairs, membership dues, and subscriptions to be greatly reduced. As the old song goes, "I am a man of means by no means; ain't got no union dues."

Floyd drove out of town in his automobile, but he was extremely careful to pay his insurance and license fees one year in advance. He rode around on out-of-state licenses at his new location, which he admits could have been risky. Most new IDers will sell their vehicle and buy a new vehicle at another location for cash, obtaining a new registration and license plates. In most states you don't have to show an ID to do this. A computer-generated bill of sale showing that you have paid sales tax is generally all that is required. Check on local requirements at the department of motor vehicles. Vehicle insurance will be expensive, but most new IDers carry just the minimum to keep them out of trouble in the event of an inadvertent crash. If the agent seems curious as to why you had no prior insurance, explain that you were overseas in the air force for four years and show him your bogus international driver's license.

Some supercautious new IDers recommend selling the vehicle where you are now for cash and riding out of town on a public carrier under an assumed name. Go to a large city with which you have no associations and then use another assumed name to buy another vehicle to travel to your final destination, they say. Computer-generated documents make the process of assuming one name after another easy and fun. On the other hand, the sheer volume of essential computers, clothes, books, files, and records you must take with you may preclude leaving town on public transportation, or, in an emergency, your leaving may be so sudden that public transportation won't work.

As stated earlier, Floyd intended to return eventually but didn't know when. He was hopeful that his vehicle and its paper cover would not expire before the registration did. In this regard, his plan may have been a bit thin. Rather than risking driving a vehicle with expired tags, he intended to abandon or sell the vehicle. This might have worked since no one important knew for sure which vehicle he left town in, and the vehicle was not the subject of a nationwide search. Others may have to be much more devious.

The point of all of this is to get aspiring new IDers to think about their transportation and their vehicle. When really deep cover is required involving federal agencies or whatever, a person cannot leave town in his original vehicle, nor can he drive around in it at his new home. Budget for a different vehicle in which to leave town, as appropriate.

Keep in mind that this is definitely not the time to celebrate your new-found freedom by purchasing a fire-engine-red convertible. Purchase a small, inconspicuous vehicle of a type common in your new city of residence. Several successful new IDers suggest purchasing a small three- or four-year-old pickup. In all cases, replacement vehicles must not reflect your old personality.

What happens if there simply isn't enough cash to do the project in the proscribed manner? If it won't hopelessly and needlessly lengthen your rap sheet, consider using checks or credit cards to raise cash, but only in your original place of residence. Doing something like this in your new city will quickly and foolishly blow your cover. One successful new IDer raised funds for his departure by cashing in the insurance policy his ex-wife received as a wedding present. Another sold his former wife's car.

Stereos, guns, sporting goods, and other valuable items should be turned into cash. Jerry, the fellow who went to the South Seas, even had a company retirement policy that he successfully cashed well before anyone really believed he was going to disappear.

Most people in our culture can quietly beg or borrow enough walking money to cover a modest year-long escape budget, if they must. If not, it may be necessary to do as the small-town gamblers did—stay where you are and stand the consequences.

# 3

# NEW ID MAKEOVERS

The following is not an unusual assignment for private investigators, or at least it isn't for me. And, even though it doesn't involve a case of new identity, it does illustrate just how difficult it is for anyone to stay hidden from people who have the resources and motivation to find him—or her, in this case.

"We want you to find Buffy," the attorneys said to me. Her real name, address, or anything else about her was unknown, except that she was witness to an angry exchange of words some two years earlier. No one connected with the incident had seen her for at least 20 months, but as one attorney instructed: "We need her statement relative to that incident, and we definitely need it by the end of the week."

In this real-life example Buffy was not trying to hide. She had no idea that she had material information about a quarter-million-dollar personal injury suit. My partner and I were to locate her using the flimsiest of evidence.

According to neighbors, Buffy lived in a low-end, low-rent section of the city for about two months with her two children. Her landlord had no record of her real name, relatives, where she had come from, or where she moved. He suspected that she might have frequented some of the bars in the city, but this is all we had to go on.

Fortunately for me, we actually found her by using only this little bit of information: I had bragged to my clients that I could find her even if she had moved to London, as long as they were willing to pay the bill. We were able to locate her in such a short time because Buffy was a creature of habit, and she did not know that someone was looking for her so she was not trying to remain "unfound." Locating her was not a particularly difficult exercise.

Reasoning that because she probably married frequently as a means of support, we looked first in all of the singles bars in the area. We had no physical description, but a bartender at the third joint we visited recognized the nickname and provided a physical description. At the time, this alone seemed something of a breakthrough to our clients. At the sixth bar, an assistant manager said that she had worked briefly as a waitress at the adjoining restaurant.

Uncharacteristically, the manager of the restaurant had a name and address, but, of course, Buffy no longer lived at that address or had that name. After only a modest amount of additional research, we uncovered her maiden name. After that, I simply called bars and restaurants and described her to whoever answered the phone until we found her sitting in one. All in all it took about five hours.

I have proved that this sort of people tracking can be done and can cite three examples of relatively easy success within the last year. In each case, I had nothing more to go on except a nickname or obscure information such as "he drove a red Ford truck," or "she runs radio-controlled model boats."

Obviously, there are many things that must be done before assuming a new ID. One vital step is to make an irrevocable personal commitment *not* to do a half-assed job. This will include purchasing *all* (not most) of the different books and videos available from Paladin, Delta, and Loompanics on skip tracing. These include the following:

1. *PI School* by Wayne Harrison (available from Paladin Press)
2. *Digital Privacy* by M.L. Shannon (available from Paladin Press)
3. *People Tracking, the Video* with Lee Lapin (available from Paladin Press)
4. *IRS Investigator's Handbook* (available from Paladin Press)
5. *SpyGame* by Scott French and Lee Lapin (available from Paladin Press)
6. *Private Eyes* by Sam Brown and Gini Scott (available from Paladin Press)
7. *You, Too, Can Find Anybody* by Joseph Culligan (available from Paladin Press)
8. *Missing Persons*, U.S.A. by Roger Willard (available from Paladin Press)
9. *Secrets of Successful Process Serving* by Nelson Tucker (available from Paladin Press)
10. *How to Find Missing Persons* by Ronald Ericksen (available from Paladin Press)
11. *Detective's Private Investigation Training Manual* by William Patterson (available from Paladin Press)

Read everything you can find on new ID before you make any plans to disappear. Many of the books are available from Paladin Press.

12. *Finder's Fee* by Ralph Thomas (available from Paladin Press)
13. *How to Investigate by Computer* by Ralph Thomas (available from Paladin Press)

*Disguise Techniques* and *Methods of Disguise* are two excellent sources of information on disguises that work.

14. *How to Find Anyone, Anywhere* by Ralph Thomas (available from Paladin Press)
15. *Find 'em Fast* by John D. McCann (available from Paladin Press)

There are many more of these books and videos. Some contain overlapping or identical information, but successful new IDers must have all the information regarding tricks that investigators use firmly in mind well before disappearing.

Being creatures of habit with predictable ways of doing things makes us easy prey for investigators, both public and private. As an example, a new IDer who subscribes to hunting magazines, has kids in school, is a horse enthusiast, has tattoos, or can't completely break contact with family members will quickly be found.

Other than including a gentle reminder that the information is available, it is not my plan to reproduce ideas available in other places. In that regard, all new IDers should secure as many books as possible on disguises. There aren't a great number, and they tend to be philosophical, making them even more valuable. I recommend *Disguise Techniques* by Edmond MacInaugh and *Methods of Disguise* by John Sample (both available from Paladin Press).

There are certainly other books of this same nature that I don't know about, and if you run across them, add them to your library. They can't help but be valuable.

We now have two completely different sets of information vital to helping the new IDer make over his physical presence and his understanding by whatever means and devices professionals will use to try to track him down.

About three weeks ago I spotted good old Darrell Posit walking through town. In 1976 he left our community, and I hadn't seen him since. Darrell wasn't a particularly good friend, but I recognized him instantly. There was more weight and more of an ambling, old man's gait, but the stooped shoulders, short brown (now graying) hair, and wool sweater worn over a cotton dress shirt gave him away even from a hundred yards.

The moral? It isn't only what a person does or where he goes, it's also what he wears, how he acts, and what his interests are. As an example, I once found a snatched kid by reviewing his grandmother's phone records. They listed calls from a medium-sized city in the Pacific Northwest. When I went to the city in another state, his mother stood out like a beacon because of the flowery, old-fashioned "granny" dresses she liked to wear. I simply hung around flea and farmers' markets till she appeared.

It is critical that one do a complete, thorough makeover before attempting a new ID. Experts suggest that at a minimum, new IDers must realistically alter the "big four": occupation, religion, hobbies, and life-style. Recall that Buffy was relatively easy to find because all she could do was work as a kind of high-level hooker.

The problem for new IDers—and an advantage

for investigators—is that everyone has one or two unique identifying characteristics that are very difficult to change.

To stay hidden, you must mint a totally new you, and changing your line of employment is the most important. An estimated 40 percent of skips are located because they mention to a relative or friend that they think X is a nice place and then go there to work in the same field as they were in before. It is so easy for an investigator to check employment in a suspected new location that it is almost criminal. You are now a computer geek? In your new life you will probably have to work construction or in a service field.

Some of these switches you will be forced to make are extremely complex. If you have kids in school and take them with you, they must now be home schooled. "Impossible," you say. But I have traced kids to other schools simply by calling regional school teachers to ask if a little, blond, second grade girl or a red-headed, thin, sixth grade boy by any name has recently enrolled in their classes. It sounds hokey, but given enough initiative and a bit of good luck, a persistent investigator will usually find the missing parents through their kids. Because of this, I have always thought that the snatched-kid syndrome was overblown. The only reason I failed to find the kids for which I was engaged to look was because the parent paying me ran out of money for or interest in the investigation.

"But I don't have kids," many new IDers say. Yet the principles are identical. An astute investigator will look for one or two pertinent bits of information relative to areas of your life that you will not easily leave behind. One investigator located a woman by checking hairdressers, for instance.

If feasible, you might consider changing your identity to that of a woman or—in the case of woman—to a man (which as a practical matter is usually much easier). If you are overweight, it may be necessary to lose a lot of weight. Or you might have to put a stone in one shoe and limp or start using artificial tanning lotions in an effort to ruddy up your complexion Do you or your girlfriend require an unusual medication? Count on ordering it mail order from Great Britain or Greece.

You must leave behind the clothes you previously wore and change your style. If you shopped at Bloomingdales, you must now make all your purchases at K-Mart. If your clothing was sloppy, loose-fitting casual, you must now select well-fitting, tailored styles—assuming you remain the same sex.

There can be no more subscriptions to *Shotgun News*, orders from Paladin Press, or membership in the American Association of Organic Farmers. Even your religious activities must be changed. Those who didn't attend church before are going to have to become enthusiastic church attendees in their new ID. Let's say you were active in the Mormon church, contributing regularly to its cause. In your new life you cannot even be a Baptist! If your need for social service is overwhelming, probably the most you could do is to join a service club such as Rotary or Kiwanis.

There will be no more shooting at the gun club or working as a volunteer in narrowly focused organizations, such as the local Friends of the Earth Society. Doing your job correctly may even entail joining the other raper-of-the-earth side of the issue. However, in all cases keep a low profile. High-profile situations that may possibly have you on CNN at the barricades where you will be recognized by an ex-spouse are definitely out. This is why so many new IDers suggest chess, stamps, or photography.

If you used to drink dark beer in bars and Diet Coke at home, fly model airplanes, frequent pornography shops, buy Schubert tapes and classic movies, wear flannel shirts, or drive a pickup, you must now abandon all these. One fellow found a person who had skipped by contacting all of the Big and Tall Stores in an area he thought this especially large fellow might have gone.

You like to drive older-model Chevrolet cars and continue to do so after you relocate, and I will find you. Switch to a yuppie-type Saab or Volvo, and it's a whole different ball game. The same applies to those who can't leave their pickups or motorcycles behind.

Only private pilots willing to make up a whole new pilot's license, complete with bogus medical certificates, are safe. Active pilots who don't change their names and numbers are dead meat. Even those who do change their documentation will fall to a determined investigator who is willing to work a day or two calling fixed-base operators at various airports.

Keep in mind that modern fax machines make it deadly simple to fire around pictures electronically and ask whether this person bought motorcycle parts, had her hair done, or was treated for a fairly unusual condition. We recently "got" a hound man a thousand miles away in Kentucky as a result of faxing his picture back to local breeders.

In addition to employment, schooling, clothing, and life-style, new IDers must be very coy about signing up for phone and utilities at their new location. Another investigator, contemplating the tasks ahead for a new IDer, said he would never fill out a change of residence form, apply for any kind of welfare, hook up to utilities even in his new name right away, or apply for a new phone number. Wait at least four to six months for these, he advised. Inconvenient, yes, but also vitally necessary.

Ignoring postal service forwarding services seems obvious, but these other precautions seem extreme unless you are in very deep trouble, and those pursuing you are very skilled and determined. However, one investigator did cite the example of a frustrated marine who took only his TV with him on his way to a new ID. Investigators found him so quickly it was ridiculous. They simply called cable TV companies in his state of birth.

People unwilling to change are quickly uncovered by tracking them through professional certificates, licenses, or obscure memberships they may have held, explaining why younger people who have not established many of these ties lose themselves will greater impunity.

Are we being too paranoid about such things? There are, after all, about 250 million Americans. Seems like, somehow, one could drop into the proverbial black hole. My friend, the chief inspector of the state police in a large Midwestern state, cities another example.

VISA, the credit card firm, now has a very large, sophisticated computer program specifically designed to spot fraudulent credit card transactions. Instantaneously, when requests for credit card authorization come in, their computers check to see whether the purchase is logical for that special cardholder. In other words, has an owner who traditionally purchased books and camping-related items suddenly decided to charge an expensive motorcycle or a massage with her card? Is the purchase logical for that area, the computer asks itself. Five grand worth of jewelry purchased by an otherwise conservative owner in Fort Wayne, Indiana, might look suspicious. "Is that purchase logical for that store?" the computer reasons. "Is it likely that firearms will be purchased in a computer store?"

The results are not perfect, but reportedly VISA's losses because of fraudulent and stolen cards were cut by about 17 percent in 1994 alone! One must assume that these programs are becoming more and more sophisticated, based on continually expanding raw data banks. Successfully relocating is far from hopeless, but aspiring new IDers can begin to see that the same remarkable technology that gives them a measure of freedom also works to take it away. This explains, in part, why a homemade death certificate may be your best defense.

New ID Metromail Corporation of Lombard, Illinois, maintains a list of 140 million Americans. Anyone can call the company's number, 1-900-288-3020, and for $3 per minute receive information regarding an individual's address, age, wife's name and age, length of current residence, median income, and even house value. Several other national data banks are also available. They do instant skip tracing based on no more than a Social Security number and name. Currently, these other firms offer their services only to professional skip tracers at high initial subscription rates. Many investigators believe that the day will quickly be upon us when anyone can dial a 900 number and be charged a nominal fee to find anyone. The shortcoming of these services is the fact that all these companies are doing is taking massive daily data collections and collating them into their data banks by name, Social Security number, place of residence, hobbies and interests, and past demographics (e.g., occupation and income).

As emphasized over and over, this does not mean that assuming a new ID is impossible or even very difficult, providing that you use modern technology, are continually cautious about getting into various data banks, and are willing to plan intelligently. Additionally, you must not be a major target for the authorities. Anyone with a file of personal data can eventually be found in our world. The real trick is to make the process so lengthy and convoluted that the game is not worth the candle.

# 4

# COMPUTER SYSTEMS

I watched in amazement as my friend the computer guru took the eyes from a color picture of a penguin he had in his computer memory and adroitly placed them into the heads of members of an office staff photo. When he finished, they looked kind of weird—almost okay, except the composite had an Orphan Annie cast to it.

Apparently my amazement was transparent and enjoyable. For his next trick, he called up a paintbrush icon and started to remove the swimsuit from the picture of a model he had copied from the Internet. Fortunately, I got him back on the subject of home-manufacturing documents before he was forced to tax his imagination unduly.

In computer land they call it desktop publishing, often referred to simply as DTP. All of us are aware that computers have completely changed how we do virtually everything. This technology has been around for quite a while, but for practical purposes, it was not as accessible to the rank and file as it is now. With the significant cost reductions of the past few years, all of this sophisticated equipment is now within financial reach of practically anyone. And function has been dumbed down (or standardized, if you prefer) so that just about anyone can run this equipment.

A close friend in the publishing business, for example, purchased a state-of-the-art computer publishing system eight years ago. He had a scanner to "read" typewritten pages into the computer. He could not scan photos with that first antique system, so the text stored required virtually no memory, and sophisticated editing, photo captioning, and other graphics manipulation were easy with what was the state-of-the-art software at the time (not Photoshop). The system cost about $40,000 for both hardware and software, and it took an experienced computer guru several months to get the system hooked up and running without operational glitches. A good part of his time was spent training the staff in how to take advantage of all this remarkable new technology.

A couple of years ago, the *Wall Street Journal* ran a feature story bemoaning the fact that professional scam artists were using $10,000 to $12,000 computer systems to rob banks. Operators used computer scanners and color printers to produce corporate stationery, driver's licenses, picture IDs of all kinds, birth certificates, and replicas of corporate checks. Company logos were stored and manipulated to suit users. In other instances, secondhand prescription forms were scanned, the writing electronically erased, and new, blank prescriptions produced with printing press accuracy without incurring the expense or risk of having the forms printed.

Crooks quickly found that it was quicker and easier

to go into the bank with homemade corporate checks that they cashed or deposited, as well as "official" letters on corporate letterhead authorizing withdrawals or transfers, than to attempt armed robbery. Banks, the *Journal* pointed out, are closed-mouthed about their losses but probably lose in the hundreds of millions annually. Pharmacists have had to resort to calling issuers of prescriptions for certain narcotics before filling orders.

To do your own documents you need a desktop publishing system consisting of a computer, a scanner, software, and a color printer. The specific recommendations that follow are meant only as a place to begin researching computer systems. The idea is to get potential new IDers thinking about this work, not to send them off in search of specific brands. Those assembling their first system simply should go into a large local computer discount warehouse such as Future Store, Computer Warehouse, or Office Max to see firsthand what is on special. Most computer store clerks will have specific, up-

To reproduce new ID documents you'll need a computer system consisting of a computer, scanner, editing software, and color printer.

to-the-minute recommendations that will undoubtedly be cheaper, faster, and better.

You may end up with something entirely different from what is listed here. The main thing is to be sure that everything will link together, without requiring that you have a Ph.D. in computer engineering, and that the three major hardware components and one software component are there. Just be sure the clerk is available on an hourly basis to come to your office to get the system fired up if it becomes necessary. A scanner I purchased specifically for my new ID process was repeatedly advertised to work on the specific make and model of my computer. However, as is still common, it would not hook to the computer. Trying to establish that this scanner would not work and return it for a refund was a horrible hassle.

## COMPUTER

Purchase a fairly heavy-duty personal computer capable of running all the peripheral machines. Computer imaging takes quite a lot of memory, and if you do not purchase a fast machine, document production will be slower than a snail at a crawl. If you intend to put many other software programs on the machine, bite the bullet and purchase a memory upgrade.

Look for a computer that has a 486 chip and at least a 66-megahertz electrical system; 120 MHz are even better, but you may find a slightly slower last-year's model at a greatly reduced price. Megahertz has to do with internal capacity for speed, memory storage retrieval, and the ability of the electronic circuit to push power through the system.

Computer memory, or the ability to store information, comes in two types. Broadly these are *random access memory (RAM)*, which the machine uses to store information used on a regular basis, such as computer programs, and *read-only memory (ROM)*, which is stored on the hard disk and is a kind of library to which the computer refers.

Your computer should have at least 16 megabytes (MB, or "megs") of RAM and a minimum of 540 megs of hard drive. By today's standards this is a limited machine, but it is adequate for sourcing documents. Sixteen MB of RAM and 540 MB of hard drive ROM will run both scanner and printer programs and allow storage of a huge number of documents.

At any given time a new IDer may need eight or ten different business cards, dozens of logos, six or eight birth certificates, several receipt blanks from doctors' offices, dozens of level-one documents (including library, union, buyer's club and church membership cards), tax documents, eight or ten state driver's licenses, dozens of credit card forms, numerous award certificates, and diplomas on the computer. The successful new IDer will voraciously scan and stock any documents within his grasp for future use.

What has been described so far is actually a fairly

A top-quality color monitor is essential to reproducing top-quality identity documents.

An older, old-fashioned, but still adequate computer can be purchased for about $1,000.

old-fashioned system. It does not include—nor do you need—a sound board, CD ROM, or mouse, but you might decide to add those. An excellent-quality color screen, however, is essential. The color balance capacity of editing programs is seriously minimized if the screen defines color poorly.

Bulk discounters buy up surplus computers from manufacturers who have to move them quickly to stay ahead of technology. They are placed on retail shelves at deep discounts. One man recently purchased an off-brand IBM clone, as illustrated above, from Wal-Mart for less than $1,000!

It was completely loaded with necessary programs; he simply took it out of the box and plugged it in, and it worked like a champ. Even a few years ago this was impossible. Computers receive their commands through software programs; the most common one now is Windows, which makes the computer menu-driven (i.e., through a series of pull-down menus, the computer will "tell" you what to do as you go along, instead of your having to type in commands as you once had to do with PCs).

## SCANNER

Now having the heart of the monster in place, it's time to add the eyes. Flatbed scanners have only recently quit being "too's": *too* expensive, *too* difficult to operate, *too* bulky and unreliable, and *too* tough to install. This has mostly changed within the past year. Some adjusting and training are still necessary to produce perfect copies, but operating the scanner is generally quick and easy.

The picture quality of a scanner is defined by dots per inch (dpi). More is better, but most printers will handle only about 600 dpi. Don't worry unduly about how dpi really works. Ask the clerk in a first-rate discount computer shop to demonstrate his color scanner output. Have prints made in both spot color, such as is sometimes used on line drawings or Christmas cards, and four color, as in color photos. By this method, it is possible to determine how well that specific scanner performs and, more important, how it couples with any given printer. Concern yourself with color quality, texture, balance, and ease of operation. But cut scanners some slack. Keep in mind that until very recently, most scanners were unreliable and extremely difficult to operate. You had to be a computer techie to make these things stand up and bark.

In some cases, large discounters carry their own brands of scanners that they discount heavily. Name brands are available, but the clones are often more salable. Unlike buying last year's computer model, which new IDers should consider, scanners must always be purchased in their very latest configuration. Expect such name brands as Hewlett-Packard, Canon, Umax, Epson, and Panasonic. There hasn't yet been enough of a market for scanners to generate "store" brands. Do not get snookered into buying a small hand-held scanner, which is much cheaper but which also doesn't work.

Cautious purchasing counts a great many points at

this time. Be certain the scanner the clerk touts will connect with the computer you have selected and that an interconnect cable is available, which often is not included with the scanner sale. It isn't the $50 or $60 as much as it is the pain in the neck involved in finding a correct connector cord or even trudging back to the same store to pick one up. A special apparatus called a SCSI (pronounced "scuzzy") card interfaces the computer to the scanner. Often this does not work. Be absolutely certain that the SCSI card comes with the scanner. If you purchase from a third-party vendor, each party will all blame the other if it doesn't work.

### SOFTWARE

Until very recently, the best editing software for scanners was sold as separate programs. The cost for a good editing program in addition to the scanner was often

Excellent brand-name scanners that sold for well over $1,000 about a year ago are now selling for under $500, and this price often includes a graphics software package.

astronomical. Currently, most scanners come complete with serviceable software, but it may not be adequate for the level of work you intend to perform and your ability. Inquire when you buy the scanner about the accompanying software and then be prepared to spend about $300 for Photoshop, the current state-of-the-art graphics-editing program. Complete packages, including scanner and program, should be about $800 to $1,000. In a year or two, they may be giving the machines and programs away with Crackerjacks.

## PRINTER

Now it's down the aisle a bit to the printer section, where we will pick out the hands of the monster. A color printer allows users to produce their own driver's licenses, library cards, medical billing forms, birth

Computer operator completes the editing of a photo to be used on an identity document and prints it on his color printer. The choice of graphics-editing software is essential to "clean up" reproduced documents and photographs. My recommendation is Photoshop.

certificates, and Social Security cards. In many cases, a color printer will even "antique" documents for makers. Coffee and tea baths may no longer be necessary.

Start by asking the clerk about the highest quality color printer he has available. Most stores will have four or five brands, including Brother, Canon, Citizen, and Epson. Almost certainly, these will be ink-jet color printers in the $400-to-$700 range, as opposed to color laser and die subliminization printers in the $2,500-to-$4,500 price bracket.

Ink-jet printers do color art very nicely. Picture quality is especially good if special coated paper sold by the printer manufacturers is used in place of plain paper. In most cases, new IDers will find this level of sophistication to be sufficient. Color photos, when required, must come from the camera and are glued into the ID separately.

Salespeople will blow lots of smoke regarding dpi, print speed, low cartridge costs, and whatnot. Don't be

A color printer is the heart of any computer system designed to produce new ID documents. An excellent color ink-jet printer can be purchased for about $500.

concerned unduly with speed and cost per copy. It won't be necessary to produce all that many documents. It is far more important that the printer reliably and accurately print color and that it handle heavy paper, Mylar, and even cover stock.

Have the clerk demonstrate color printer capability and quality, hooked to scanners he has on the floor. Look at many different examples. Put yourself in the place of a Social Security administrator who may be looking at your credentials. Is the work credible, you must ask. In some cases, it is amazing what even an extra $200 will buy in terms of a color printer. Make your purchase, accepting the fact that as soon as you walk out the door, prices will drop 25 percent for something materially better.

Some home printers work at speeds of 10 to 12 pages per minute and will print on heavy cover stock, Mylar, or even fancy coated paper. They aren't as fast as offset presses, but quality can be just as good—and speed in the ID business is not nearly as important as quality and credibility.

If you need higher quality than the ink-jet provides, laser color printers are available for rental at many of the office support shops, such as Kinko's, Office Max, Copy Court, and others springing up around the country. Or you may be forced to purchase one of the $2,500 to $4,500 Hewlett-Packard or Canon models as a last resort.

In summary, to this point you have done the following:

1. Purchased an older model new computer that is missing many bells and whistles (literally), but which has at least 16 MB of RAM and 540 MB of hard-disk storage memory (ROM).

2. Bought the latest high-resolution, 600-dpi color scanner that is guaranteed to connect to your computer.

3. Personally observed the machine scan both artist's color renditions and color photos.
4. Determined that the scanner will function with your computer and that a suitable guarantee to that effect is in place.
5. Made sure that a knowledgeable, skilled store clerk is available on a consulting basis to help with setup and initial operation.
6. Ascertained that the scanner comes with necessary operational and editing software or that these programs are available.
7. Stupid as it may sound, established that operational cords from computer to scanner are on hand.
8. Purchased a high-quality color ink-jet printer from a reputable store.
9. Secured a warranty for the printer.
10. Hooked it up to your scanner to make sure it works acceptably.
11. Scouted out print shops where you can rent expensive laser color printers if you need higher quality for some jobs.

Your desktop publishing package is now complete, including a fast computer with reasonable memory capacity costing about $900, a high-resolution scanner and software program costing about $1,000, and a high-quality color ink-jet printer at about $500. Total cost is about $2,400—unless it becomes necessary to go to a color laser printer, in which case the price theoretically more than doubles.

Even purchased in a small town with all of the laminating devices, paper cutters, and stamps, the assembled equipment will still be under $3,000! Leaving the computer budget substantially high is wise. Although the situation is dramatically improved, it has been common for parts of these systems not to work at all. In 1988, for instance, I purchased a Blaser brand laser printer that never worked at all, right out of the box. Avoid this problem by securing at least a one-year warranty from a larger dealer.

Although these computer, scanner, and printer systems are universal, you must exercise some care when purchasing them. This is especially true if you purchase a photo-grade printer at the time everything else is assembled. Desktop publishing won't generally arouse suspicion, but it might be wise to drive around town or to neighboring towns where various brand-name components are purchased one at a time for cash.

Our old friend, new IDer Ken, purchased all of his computer components a piece at a time over six months, while he still lived in his old residence. He purchased one printer (now junked) by mail order, but he cautions that without a valid, working credit card, mail order is difficult unless you elect to use the more cumbersome and uncertain method of sending a money order.

## PAPER

New IDers should shop at full-line stationery supply stores for appropriate weight, color, and quality of paper to make up various documents. In most cases, new IDers soon acquire a large stock of various kinds and weights of paper, but paper is relatively cheap. Not all stock paper that may be required is easily purchased. Some high-rag bond or coated papers are not usually carried by retail shops, or, if they are, they are in four-foot-square sheets, which must be cut into usable sizes.

It may be possible to identify new IDers by the fact that they constantly shop at the same stationery store for paper supplies. Try various stationery stores, as well as printers, schools, commercial artists, layout shops, or any other odd locations. One new IDer claimed that he found the perfect piece of paper for a form he was duplicating in a wedding invitation. He only used the unmarked bottom third of one page. It is, however, an inviolable rule of

Matching the color, texture, and weight of paper used to replicate documents to those used for originals is a constant challenge for new IDers.

computers that if you have only one piece of paper the printer will figure it out and eat your only piece of paper.

## OTHER SUPPLIES

Other small tools needed include a professional flatbed paper cutter, professional scissors, a large magnifying glass, a plastic lamination machine, and a sewing machine. Some documents, such as buyer's club cards and driver's licenses, can be made on coated paper or Mylar and laminated into plastic. Detection is difficult to impossible even though the license is not printed on official plastic material, as are the originals.

\* \* \*

You are now all set to start turning out high-quality, homemade ID documents. Turn the computer on and follow the instructions on the screen. Most modern computer programs lead you through various sequences necessary to start production. At this point new IDers are not interested in volume. Simply keep hacking away at the machine till you reach a complete impasse. Then call or visit one of the stores from which you purchased your equipment for help. If there are three different local stores to tap for information, avoid becoming a memorable pest at any one store. Nothing currently precludes anyone from pursuing desktop publishing, but obscurity is always better, if possible.

As a first task, run your ex-wife's old school record and birth certificate through the scanner. Check the computer screen to be certain a good copy was achieved. Using the editing function, lift off her name, address, sex, and other personal data. Erase any old seals. Appropriate new, raised seals must be purchased with which to "authenticate" the new document. If the document has been stamped SAMPLE or VOID, don't worry; you can erase that as well. Documents can be magnified scores of times so that line quality can be repaired where needed.

Most school records and old birth records are filled in by hand or by using an old manual typewriter. It may be necessary to go to a yard sale or hockshop to purchase a manual typewriter. Reportedly, these old hackers have become scarce, perhaps because of the number of people producing old documents. Finished forms may look better than originals, but authentic-looking defects should be retained as needed. Some birth certificates, for example, are copied out of large volumes having a kind of curled, wrap-around, "copied from a big book" effect. You can replicate this on your system.

Be sure that the paper on which the document is printed matches the original. Antiquing may not be necessary since this document may be presented as a modern certified copy of an old original.

Next, practice using the machine's various type styles and editing ability to lay out several bogus business cards, complete with the most prestigious or obscure (whichever works best) address in town. Print these on heavyweight, white cover stock. Two- or three-color type and logo add effect. Learning this process takes longer than telling about it. Most neophytes, if they take their time, find the process interesting and fascinating, especially after they begin to produce usable documents.

As emphasized over and over, determined investigation will uncover any of these documents. But thorough investigation will eventually compromise any cover, no matter how sophisticated, if the pursuers are persistent and good enough. The trick is to carry along the computer system with you to turn out additional documents for use on people who are unable or unlikely to verify them.

# 5

# LEVELS OF ID

To a great extent, we Americans are defined by a few relatively simple pieces of paper that follow us all our lives, even though we may not present most of these papers for inspection for 40 or 50 years. People simply assume that these identity papers are there in the background someplace. A corollary to this truth is that people will generally assume whatever we tell them to be the truth about ourselves, our family, and our employment. Often this assumption is made on the basis of the lowest level of ID.

For example, I have never shown any one of the four banks with which I do business a Social Security card, birth certificate, or driver's license in spite of the fact that I have opened and closed dozens of accounts over the years. In several notorious cases, I opened checking accounts in a company name using Richard Nixon's Social Security number! No one ever questioned a thing. Eight years later, I simply closed the account. Whenever I needed a Social Security number, I made one up or used Dick's.

Possession of these key documents assumes their validity, even if they are seldom used again. Their being used just one time will not diminish their importance. Shrewd new IDers must know about these documents and the role they will play in their new lives. Identity documents must be manipulated and used correctly, or they will, in and of themselves, expose the aspiring new IDer.

## LEVELS OF DOCUMENTS

Broadly, identity documents can be classified on three levels:

1. *So-called breeder documents from which most or many other important documents can eventually be acquired.* These can be forged or genuine. Given our current level of technology and a bit of diligence, one is as good as the other. The most common include a birth certificate, Social Security card, and driver's license.

2. *Intermediate-level documents that are not used exclusively to acquire other documents.* Nevertheless, they are very important for life as we know it. They might include military discharge papers; school records and diplomas; hunting and fishing licenses (which are sometimes more difficult to acquire than one might suppose); credit cards; membership cards for such organizations as the Elks, Eagles, or Farm

Bureau; marriage or divorce records; Immigration and Naturalization Service (INS) documents; vehicle and medical insurance cards; school records; pilot's licenses; international driver's licenses; IRS tax document; union cards; and occupational skill certificates. All of these are easy to make up, as needed.

3. *Documents that primarily support the others.* These are the easily acquired items handed out simply for the asking, including business cards, library cards, country club membership cards, buying club cards, and some of the many ready-made occupational cards offered by vendors. Some of these are quite fancy, having pictures, raised seals, and color art. They can be acquired in the person's assumed name directly from the club or organization, purchased from vendors, or simply turned out on a computer. About the only problem with the latter option is finding the original forms and keeping everything organized. Some professional check kiters are involved in so many scams at the same time that it takes a computer program just to keep things sorted out.

It is important to keep in mind that there is some overlap in these levels. Documents slip in and out of levels, depending entirely on the number and quality of supporting documents a person has, as well as his ability to keep track of his cover story. Most paper trip experts, for instance, don't think much of international driver's licenses. Yet some really adept users have practically elevated these documents to level one in terms of other documents they have generated with them.

Likewise, the level of acceptance also dictates

Basic stamps and seals needed to "certify" new documents can be purchased inexpensively from office supply outlets.

whether a document is level one, two, or three, and this depends in large measure on the ability and propensity of various officials to check them out. For example, a bank teller can't detect a good homemade driver's license. Acceptance often hinges on the bearer's personal appearance and demeanor, including clothes, haircut, race, eye contact, articulateness, and body language—all measured against the state of confusion in the recipient's office at the time.

### Level-One Documents

Experts acknowledge that a state-certified birth certificate, driver's license, and Social Security card with valid correlating numbers are core documents from which all others spring. Yet, if you boil it all down, what is required is a certified copy of a birth certificate, or a good copy thereof, from which to acquire a Social Security card and driver's license. Theoretically, any new IDer who can produce a certified copy of a birth certificate at home in his basement or garage has got his new ID.

## Birth Certificate

For the birth certificate, use your own, a recent spouse's, your child's, or an acquaintance's name. Sample copies of uncertified birth certificates are easily acquired from a state bureau of vital statistics or county registration office. People who are serious about the business will quickly accumulate large quantities of official blank documents to be used as computer models. State stamps used to authenticate the document are available from stationery stores or by mail from NIC Law Enforcement Supply, Box 5950, Shreveport, LA 71135.

## Social Security Number

Undoubtedly the best plan—if there is time—is to make up enough documents to apply for a new Social Security number in a new name. Children between the ages of 1 month and 5 years are granted mail-order Social Security numbers with few questions. All that is required is a certified birth certificate and one piece of collaborating documentation, which can include a doctor's or hospital bill, baptismal certificate, or copy of a government bond received from a grandparent made out in the child's name. Originals of any of these documents can be scanned into a computer and the original names edited out and the new names inserted. With a bit of practice, the procedure is as easy as writing about it.

According to Social Security Administration departmental policy, it is forbidden to divulge a person's age based on his Social Security number. Securing a Social Security number for those under the age of 5 is a simple operation handled entirely by mail, preferably to a mail drop. Although this procedure has been successful on numerous occasions, it is not foolproof. Social Security officials may smell a rat and kick the homemade birth certificate back. If all is handled through a postal box or mail drop, little is lost. Simply make another document and try again in a few weeks.

Some new IDers have been successful in going personally to the Social Security office. If the document is questioned, the petitioner simply tells the clerk, "Sorry, what you have is what the state sent me." There are an estimated 7,000 different forms of birth certificates in the United States. Most Social Security clerks have seen so many different editions of birth certificates they don't know what is correct or, in many cases, really care.

All new IDers who have tried it recently caution against trying to turn a certified birth certificate for a 45-year-old into a new Social Security number. It can be done, but not without a huge amount of suspicion, scrutiny, and investigation. And absolutely anyone over 45 who applies raises red flags. Lately, Social Security administrators have insisted on making calls to verify, talking to parents and relatives, as well as contacting the telephone company,

When applying for new ID documents, use a mail drop instead of a street address if possible. Of course, some agency officials may become suspicious of a box number and insist on a street address.

utility offices, and others who can verify the person they see in front of them. Most of this has come as a result of new laws regarding child-support payments.

Using charts found in most new ID books, makers can gin up plausible Social Security numbers for placement on driver's licenses or Social Security cards. Increasingly, however, these will not pass official scrutiny because most official data banks are tied together, including the IRS, state motor vehicle departments, welfare agencies, National Crime Information Center (NCIC), and INS. Any official check will uncover fraud. In this regard, conditions are more hostile to the new IDer than ever, especially if he is attempting to escape court-ordered child-support payments. Federal Parent Locator Services run by the Department of Health and Human Services necessitate that new IDers be more diligent than ever. Once a parent leaves, he can never use his old Social Security number again.

If used discreetly, new IDers can live for a long time on bogus Social Security numbers. Bank employees, schools, foreign border guards, and even some employers are unlikely to detect false Social Security numbers. Police agencies, the IRS, welfare offices, drivers' license bureaus, and passport offices will most likely uncover them immediately. However, at times there is some middle ground for the clever.

**Driver's License**

A ploy that has worked temporarily for some new IDers who have not had time to get a full-blown plan in motion involves manufacturing an international driver's license to use to drive to a new location. One man took a business card, library card, and an international driver's license and parlayed them into a regular driver's license in a state through which he was passing on his way to his new location. He picked a state that did not require a Social Security number for a driver's license. Later, at his final destination, he used a homemade birth certificate to acquire a Social Security number and then traded his previous state and international license for one in his new state.

## Passport

Securing a valid new-ID passport, the last item in first level of breeder IDs, is not easy. It has been done with computer-generated birth certificates, but not without anxiety and high-quality bogus documents.

Two methods for trying this are recommended. One involves applying before one's passport official in a local courthouse or post office and having the passport and birth certificate returned to a mail drop. The clerk won't detect a newly made birth certificate, but the passport people might. In this case any trace of your trail will end at the mail drop. The second method, which has also worked, involves taking one computer-generated, stamped birth certificate directly to a passport office in Boston, Chicago, Honolulu, Miami, New Orleans, New York, Philadelphia, Seattle, or Washington, D.C. Because they have seen so many poor attempts at fraud, it is not recommended that you go in person to Los Angeles or San Francisco. Take along a driver's license made up with a real Social Security number, a business card, and several library cards or backup documents. If the clerk objects to your birth certificate, simply say, "It's what they sent me. What should I ask for that's different?" It has worked recently.

Simply restricting your travel to Canada and Mexico using a homemade birth certificate may be wiser, rather than trying for a usable passport. Because of the materials involved and because of computers and scanners deployed by U.S. Customs people, producing a usable passport on a computer system is not feasible. (See pages 68–71 for a copy of a Social Security card application form and pages 72–75 for a copy of a U.S. passport application form.)

Most people are almost foolishly emboldened after working on their computer scanner equipment. Turning out good, usable documents is fun and easy, but try not to get carried away.

### Level-Two Documents
Original second-level IDs, to some small extent, can be acquired by using first-level documents, or, once you are set up, most are easy to turn out on the computer. These are official documents issued by fairly reputable organizations. Examples include bank credit cards, international driver's licenses, military cards and papers, check-cashing cards, service club memberships such as Rotary or Kiwanis, student or faculty ID cards, professional or occupational cards, and employee IDs. Of these, only credit cards are not possible on the computer scanner. Machines can be purchased that produce credit cards, but they are not common and cost about $6,000. Since our goal is to induce people to believe that we are someone else and not to scam banks out of their money, it would seem most cost-efficient to get a valid credit card from a bank by using ID produced on the scanner rather than manufacturing credit cards at home.

Level-two ID is sometimes described as photo IDs issued by private or quasi-private organizations. It is faster to make these documents at home, and chances of being caught with them are nil, but they won't work for their intended purpose within the organization. In other words, carrying a usable bank card has utility other than ID, but a counterfeit union card may have little use outside the union. One might as well make up these last types at home, using totally bogus codes and numbers, if their only purpose is to back up other ID.

Of all photo documents, international driver's licenses are the easiest to fabricate. All it takes is a photocopier and a red pencil. Other than for hit-and-run accidents or drunken driving arrests, users have been 100-percent successful with these documents by telling officers that all their other pieces of identification were in their camera case, which was stolen while returning from a work assignment overseas. But, they go on to say, they are on their way to the state university to study and will, within a day or two, get a real driver's license. This ploy has bought users some time and distance when first leaving, but if the officer checks the vehicle insurance and registration, which won't match the bogus name you have placed on the license, you're caught. Of course, you could also easily make insurance and registration on a computer, but, unlike international driver's licenses, they can be verified by the dispatcher.

Doing a finished job on level-two ID may require purchasing a laminating machine or using one at a local copying shop, such as Kinko's.

### Level-Three Documents

Level-three IDs are usually defined as those not having either a picture or Social Security number. Often they don't even have an office code on them. The rule of thumb is that these documents are far more valuable than most people who have never used them suppose. People generally want to believe you are who and what you say you are. If all that is available is a voter's ID card; old tax return; or library, insurance, buyer's club, or business card, they will accept that. It is about a 50-50 deal whether these come from their original issuer or from the computer. Once the form is scanned into the computer, it is there until you delete it. Some desktop producers conveniently find themselves with quite a few different documents from which to choose.

At times, these IDs are successfully used as stand-alones, but generally they work best in conjunction with other documents. On several occasions, I have gotten past U.S. Customs people by using home-grown business cards. Little did they know that once they had my business card, there were only three more like it in the entire world.

Current electronic-age new IDers question the utility of private mail drops. Private owners, they point out, will provide information to investigators as quickly as post office employees.

Several people have asked me about which is better, a post office box or a mail drop. "If the minute you leave your old city you become someone new and have a fine new driver's license to prove it, what difference does a mail drop versus a post office box make?"

Ken advises, "Rent a U.S. postal box or mail drop, whichever is easier. In some cases a U.S. postal box is more credible," he concludes.

Requirements for renting a postal box or mail drop are extremely lax. Minimal identification is required, and Social Security numbers are not. Even if they were, they are not cross-checked. (Sample copies of the application and rules are on pages 76–78.)

Modern mail drops are usually open 24 hours a day, but post office lobbies are generally open from 6:00 A.M. to 10:00 P.M. Once the box is open in either place, practically no one needs to see you in person again. Open the box at least six months before you expect to need it in a medium-to-large city, using computer-generated ID. No face could ever be traced under these circumstances.

Quickly fill out the form, pay a year's rent in advance in cash, dress and behave inconspicuously, and no one will probably remember you. For your home address, list either a nonexistent rural address such as R.R. 4, Box 4037, or list the largest, cheapest, cruddiest flophouse in the region. Investigators hate those poor sections of town: people filter through them like so many barn pigeons.

Some new IDers highly recommend relocating in a community that is home to an educational institution with large transient population. There is merit to that concept. New IDers can easily be lost in the crowd at a university or college. Even relatively small trade schools have significant numbers of students and faculty who move through the community yearly.

List one of their residence halls as your address on

the mail drop or postal box application form. Postal boxes taken out at university post offices are ideal. Hundreds of people crowd into what are usually small facilities daily. Because of the huge number of students coming and going, postal employees will probably not recognize pictures of you after a month or two—if it ever comes to that.

In the past, securing printed document forms of sufficient quality to do the job of producing new ID was impractical, if not impossible. Now all documents can be made at home with impunity. In most cases, these won't be compromised any more quickly or easily by determined authorities than so-called originals. An additional advantage to computer-generated documents is that they can be churned out in such large quantities so cheaply that if one doesn't work you can quickly move on to the next set and the next.

But all of this requires some rudimentary knowledge of computers, and so be sure that you learned everything in Chapter 4.

TEXAS DEPARTMENT OF HEALTH
BUREAU OF VITAL STATISTICS
1100 WEST 49TH STREET
AUSTIN, TEXAS 78756-3191
PHONE (512) 458-7111

APPLICATION FOR CERTIFIED COPY OF BIRTH OR DEATH CERTIFICATE

**BIRTH** ☐                                      **DEATH** ☐

# REQUESTED                                      # REQUESTED
_____ CERTIFIED COPIES X $11.00= _____           _____ CERTIFIED COPY X $9.00 = _____
_____ WALLET-SIZE X $11.00      = _____          _____ EXTRA COPIES X $3.00   = _____
           TOTAL ENCLOSED = _____                         TOTAL ENCLOSED = _____

**PLEASE PRINT**
See Reverse Side for Instructions

1. NAME ON
   RECORD _____
              FIRST                    MIDDLE                    LAST

2. DATE OF EVENT
   ☐ BIRTH ☐ DEATH _____          3. SEX _____
              MONTH      DAY      YEAR

4. PLACE OF
   EVENT _____
           CITY          or        COUNTY

5. FATHER'S
   NAME _____
              FIRST                    MIDDLE                    LAST

6. MOTHER'S
   MAIDEN NAME _____
              FIRST                    MIDDLE                    LAST

7. ADDITIONAL IDENTIFYING INFORMATION FOR <u>DEATH</u> CERTIFICATE.

   SOCIAL SECURITY NUMBER OF DECEASED _____

   BIRTH DATE _____

   BIRTH PLACE, ETC. _____

8. APPLICANT'S NAME: _____ 9. TELEPHONE #: (____) _____
                                                               (MON-FRI 8:00-5:00)

10. MAILING ADDRESS: _____
                     STREET ADDRESS              CITY        STATE        ZIP

11. RELATIONSHIP TO PERSON NAMED IN ITEM 1: _____

12. PURPOSE FOR OBTAINING THIS RECORD: _____

   **WARNING: THE PENALTY FOR KNOWINGLY MAKING A FALSE STATEMENT IN THIS FORM CAN BE 2-10 YEARS
   IN PRISON AND A FINE OF UP TO $10,000. (HEALTH AND SAFETY CODE, CHAPTER 678, SEC.195.003)**

_____          _____
SIGNATURE OF APPLICANT                    DATE

IDENTIFICATION TYPE _____       NUMBER _____
ATTACH PHOTOCOPY
         Drivers License, I.D. Card, etc.          on Drivers License, I.D. Card, etc

FEES ARE SUBJECT TO CHANGE WITHOUT NOTICE (CALL 512-458-7111 FOR FEE VERIFICATION). THE SEARCHING OR
INDEXING FEE IS NON-REFUNDABLE EVEN IF A RECORD IS NOT FOUND.

BIRTH RECORDS ARE CONFIDENTIAL FOR 50 YEARS AND DEATH RECORDS ARE CONFIDENTIAL FOR 25 YEARS; THERE-
FORE, ISSUANCE IS RESTRICTED. OTHER RECORDS MAY BE OBTAINED WHEN SUFFICIENT INFORMATION FOR IDENTIFICA-
TION IS PROVIDED. PLEASE ATTACH A PHOTOCOPY OF ID TO APPLICATION.

ADMINISTRATIVE RULES REQUIRE THAT ON RESTRICTED RECORDS, ALL IDENTIFYING INFORMATION (ITEMS 1-5), RELA-
TIONSHIP (ITEM 10), AND PURPOSE (ITEM 11) BE PROVIDED IN ORDER TO ISSUE THE RECORD.

VS-141 REV 1293

State of Texas application for certified copy of birth or death certificate.

## SOCIAL SECURITY ADMINISTRATION
Application for a Social Security Card

Inside is the form you need to apply for a Social Security card. You can also use this form to replace a lost card or to change your name on your card. This service is free. But before you go on to the form, please read through the rest of this page. We want to cover some facts you should know before you apply.

| | |
|---|---|
| **IF YOU HAVE NEVER HAD A SOCIAL SECURITY NUMBER**  | If you were born in the U.S. and have never had a Social Security number, you must complete this form and show us documents that show your age, citizenship, and who you are. Usually, all we need from you are:<br><br>• Your birth certificate; AND<br>• Some form of identity, such as a driver's license, school record, or medical record. See page 2 for more examples.<br><br>We prefer to see your birth certificate. However, we will accept a hospital record of your birth made before you were 5 years old, or a religious record of your age or birth made before you were 3 months old. **We must see original documents or certified copies. Uncertified photocopies are not acceptable.** You may apply at any age, but if you are 18 or older when you apply for your first Social Security card, **you must apply in person. Please see the special requirements on page 4 if you were born outside the U.S., if you are not a U.S. citizen or if you need a card for a child.** |
| **IF YOU NEED TO REPLACE YOUR CARD** | To replace your card, all we usually need is one type of identification and this completed form. See page 2 for examples of documents we will accept. If you were born outside the U.S., you must also submit proof of U.S. citizenship or lawful alien status. Examples of the documents we will accept are on page 4. **Remember, we must see original documents or certified copies.** |
| **IF YOU NEED TO CHANGE YOUR NAME ON YOUR CARD** | If you already have a number, but need to change your name on our records, we need this completed form and a document that identifies you by both your old and new names. Examples include a marriage certificate, a divorce decree or a court order that changes your name. Or, we will accept two documents—one with your old name and one with your new name. See page 2 for examples of documents we will accept. If you were born outside the U.S., you must also show proof of U.S. citizenship or lawful alien status. Examples of documents we will accept are on page 4. |
| **HOW TO APPLY** | First complete this form, using the instructions on page 2. Then take or mail it to the nearest Social Security office. Be sure to take or mail the originals or certified copies of your documents along with the form. We will return your documents right away. |
| **IF YOU HAVE ANY QUESTIONS** | If you have any questions about this form, or about the documents you need to show us, please contact any Social Security office. A telephone call will help you make sure you have everything you need to apply for your card. |

Form SS-5 (9/89) 5/88 edition may be used until supply is exhausted

Application for a Social Security card.

| DOCUMENTS THAT SHOW YOUR IDENTITY | Here are some examples of identity documents that we will accept. |

- Driver's license
- U.S. government or state employee ID card
- Your passport
- School ID card, record, or report card
- Marriage or divorce record
- Health insurance card

- Clinic, doctor, or hospital records
- Military records
- Court order for name change
- Adoption records
- Church membership or confirmation record (if not used as evidence of age)
- Insurance policy

We will NOT accept a birth certificate or hospital record as proof of your identity. We will accept other documents if they have enough information to identify you. **Remember, we must see original documents or copies certified by the county clerk or other official who keeps the record.**

| HOW TO COMPLETE THE FORM | Most questions on the form are self-explanatory. The questions that need explanation are discussed below. The numbers match the numbered questions on the form. **If you are completing this form for someone else, please answer the questions as they apply to that person.** Then, sign your own name in question 16. |

1. Your card will show your full first, middle, and last names **unless you show otherwise.** If you have ever used another name, show it on the third line. You can show more than one name on this line. Do not show a nickname unless you have used it for work or business.

2. Show the address where you want your card mailed. If you do not usually get mail at this address, please show an "in care of address", for example, c/o John Doe, 1 Elm Street, Anytown, U.S.A. 00000.

3. If you check "other" under Citizenship, please attach a statement that explains your situation and why you need a Social Security number.

5. You do not have to answer our question about race/ethnic background. We can issue you a Social Security card without this information. However, this information is important. We use it to study and report on how Social Security programs affect different people in our nation. Of course, we use it only for statistical reports and do not reveal the identities of individuals.

13. If the date of birth you show in item 6 is different from the date of birth you used on an earlier application, show the date of birth you used on the earlier application on this line.

16. If you cannot sign your name, sign with an "X" mark and have two people sign beneath your mark as witnesses.

Form SS-5 (9/89)

2

# SOCIAL SECURITY ADMINISTRATION
## Application for a Social Security Card

Form Approved
OMB No. 0960-0066

**INSTRUCTIONS**

- Please read "How To Complete This Form" on page 2.
- Print or type using black or blue ink. DO NOT USE PENCIL.
- After you complete this form, take or mail it along with the required documents to your nearest Social Security office.
- If you are completing this form for someone else, answer the questions as they apply to that person. Then, sign your name in question 16.

**1 NAME**
To Be Shown On Card

FIRST     FULL MIDDLE NAME     LAST

FULL NAME AT BIRTH
IF OTHER THAN ABOVE    FIRST     FULL MIDDLE NAME     LAST

OTHER NAMES USED

**2 MAILING ADDRESS**
Do Not Abbreviate

STREET ADDRESS, APT. NO., PO BOX, RURAL ROUTE NO.

CITY     STATE     ZIP CODE

**3 CITIZENSHIP**
(Check One)

☐ U.S. Citizen   ☐ Legal Alien Allowed To Work   ☐ Legal Alien Not Allowed To Work   ☐ Foreign Student Allowed Restricted Employment   ☐ Conditionally Legalized Alien Allowed To Work   ☐ Other (See Instructions On Page 2)

**4 SEX**

☐ Male    ☐ Female

**5 RACE/ETHNIC DESCRIPTION**
(Check One Only—Voluntary)

☐ Asian, Asian-American Or Pacific Islander   ☐ Hispanic   ☐ Black (Not Hispanic)   ☐ North American Indian Or Alaskan Native   ☐ White (Not Hispanic)

**6 DATE OF BIRTH**
MONTH DAY YEAR

**7 PLACE OF BIRTH**
(Do Not Abbreviate)
CITY   STATE OR FOREIGN COUNTRY   FCI

Office Use Only

**8 MOTHER'S MAIDEN NAME**
FIRST     FULL MIDDLE NAME     LAST NAME AT HER BIRTH

**9 FATHER'S NAME**
FIRST     FULL MIDDLE NAME     LAST

**10** Has the person in item 1 ever received a Social Security number before?

☐ Yes (If "yes", answer questions 11-13.)    ☐ No (If "no", go on to question 14.)    ☐ Don't Know (If "don't know", go on to question 14.

**11** Enter the Social Security number previously assigned to the person listed in item 1.

☐☐☐ – ☐☐ – ☐☐☐☐

**12** Enter the name shown on the most recent Social Security card issued for the person listed in item 1.

FIRST     MIDDLE     LAST

**13** Enter any different date of birth if used on an earlier application for a card.   MONTH DAY YEAR

**14 TODAY'S DATE** ▶ MONTH DAY YEAR    **15 DAYTIME PHONE NUMBER** ▶ ( ) AREA CODE

DELIBERATELY FURNISHING (OR CAUSING TO BE FURNISHED) FALSE INFORMATION ON THIS APPLICATION IS A CRIME PUNISHABLE BY FINE OR IMPRISONMENT, OR BOTH

**16 YOUR SIGNATURE** ▶    **17 YOUR RELATIONSHIP TO THE PERSON IN ITEM 1 IS:**

☐ Self   ☐ Natural Or Adoptive Parent   ☐ Legal Guardian   ☐ Other (Specify)

| DO NOT WRITE BELOW THIS LINE (FOR SSA USE ONLY) | | | | | | |
|---|---|---|---|---|---|---|
| NPN | | | DOC | NTI | CAN | ITV |
| PBC | EVI | EVA | EVC | PRA | NWR | DNR | UNIT |
| EVIDENCE SUBMITTED | | | | | SIGNATURE AND TITLE OF EMPLOYEE(S) REVIEWING EVIDENCE AND OR CONDUCTING INTERVIEW | |
| | | | | | | DATE |
| | | | DCL | | | DATE |

Form SS-5 (9/89) 5/88 edition may be used until supply is exhausted

| IF YOU ARE A UNITED STATES CITIZEN BORN OUTSIDE THE U.S. | If you are a United States citizen who was born outside the U.S., we need to see your consular report of birth (FS-240 or FS-545), if you have one. We also need to see one form of identification. See page 2 for examples of identity documents we will accept. |
|---|---|

If you do not have your consular report of birth, we will need to see your foreign birth certificate and one of the following: a U.S. Citizen ID card, U.S. passport, Certificate of Citizenship, or a Certificate of Naturalization. Remember, you must show us the original documents.

| IF YOU ARE NOT A U.S. CITIZEN | If you are not a U.S. citizen, you must show us your birth certificate or passport, and the documents given to you by the Immigration and Naturalization Service (INS). **We must see original documents, not photocopies.** Examples of INS documents are: your Alien Registration Receipt Card (Form I-151 or I-551) or Form I-94. Because these documents should not be mailed, you should apply in person. |
|---|---|

Even though you may not be authorized to work in this country, we can issue you a Social Security card if you are here legally and need it for some other reason. Your card will be marked to show that you cannot work, and if you do, we will notify INS.

| IF YOU NEED A CARD FOR A CHILD OR SOMEONE ELSE | If you apply for a card for a child or someone else, you need to show us that person's original or certified birth certificate and one more document showing the person's identity. For example, for a child we will accept a doctor or hospital bill, a school record or any similar document that shows the child's identity. For an adult, see page 2 for examples of identity documents we will accept. |
|---|---|

**Also, if you sign the form, we need to see some kind of identification for you.** Please see the list on page 2 for examples of documents we will accept. Be sure to answer the questions on the application form as they apply to the person needing the card.

## THE PAPERWORK/PRIVACY ACT AND YOUR APPLICATION

The Social Security Act (sections 205(c) and 702) allows us to collect the facts we ask for on this form. We use most of these facts to assign you a Social Security number or to issue you a card. You do not have to give us these facts, but without them we cannot issue you a Social Security number or a card. Without a number, you could lose Social Security benefits in the future and you might not be able to get a job.

We give out the facts on this form without your consent only in certain situations that are explained in the Federal Register. For example, we must give out this information if Federal law requires us to, if your Congressman or Senator needs the information to answer questions you ask them, or if the Justice Department needs it to investigate and prosecute violations of the Social Security Act.

We may also use the information you give us when we match records by computer. Matching programs compare our

records with those of other Federal, State, or local government agencies. Many agencies may use matching programs to find or prove that a person qualifies for benefits paid by the Federal government. The law allows us to do this even if you do not agree to it. If you would like more facts about the Privacy Act, get in touch with any Social Security office.

We estimate that it will take you about 8 minutes to complete this form. This includes the time it will take to read the instructions, gather the necessary facts and fill out the form. If you have comments or suggestions on how long it takes to complete this form or on any other aspect of this form, write to the Social Security Administration, ATTN: Reports Clearance Officer, 1-A-21 Operations Bldg., Baltimore, MD 21235, and to the Office of Management and Budget, Paperwork Reduction Project (0960-0066), Washington, D.C. 20503. **Do not send completed forms or information concerning your claim to these offices.**

Form SS-5 (9/89)       "U.S. Government Printing Office: 1994 — 377-589

4

UNITED STATES DEPARTMENT OF STATE

**APPLICATION FOR** ☐ **PASSPORT** ☐ **REGISTRATION**

SEE INSTRUCTIONS—TYPE OR PRINT IN INK IN WHITE AREAS

**1. NAME** FIRST NAME     MIDDLE NAME

LAST NAME

**2. MAILING ADDRESS**

STREET

CITY, STATE, ZIP CODE

COUNTRY     IN CARE OF

☐ 5 Yr. ☐ 10 Yr.   Issue
R   D   O   DP   Date _____
End. # _____   Exp. _____

**3. SEX**    **4. PLACE OF BIRTH** City, State or Province, Country   **5. DATE OF BIRTH**   **6.** SEE FEDERAL TAX SOCIAL SECURITY NUMBER

Male   Female     Mo.   Day   Year    LAW NOTICE ON REVERSE SIDE

**7. HEIGHT**    **8. COLOR OF HAIR**    **9. COLOR OF EYES**    **10.** (Area Code) HOME PHONE   **11.** (Area Code) BUSINESS PHO

Feet Inches    **12. PERMANENT ADDRESS** (Street, City, State, ZIP Code)      **13. OCCUPATION**

**14. FATHER'S NAME**    BIRTHPLACE    BIRTH DATE   U S CITIZEN    **16. TRAVEL PLANS** (Not Mandatory)
    ☐ YES ☐ NO   COUNTRIES     DEPARTURE DA

**15. MOTHER'S MAIDEN NAME**    BIRTHPLACE    BIRTH DATE   U S CITIZEN
    YES   NO       LENGTH OF STA

**17. HAVE YOU EVER BEEN ISSUED A U.S. PASSPORT?** YES ☐   NO ☐    IF YES, SUBMIT PASSPORT IF AVAILABLE. ☐ Submm-

IF UNABLE TO SUBMIT MOST RECENT PASSPORT, STATE ITS DISPOSITION: COMPLETE NEXT LINE

NAME IN WHICH ISSUED    PASSPORT NUMBER    ISSUE DATE (Mo., Day, Yr.)     DISPOSITION

SUBMIT TWO RECENT IDENTICAL PHOTOS

FROM 1" TO 1-3/8"

2" × 2" FROM 1" TO

**18. HAVE YOU EVER BEEN MARRIED?** ☐ YES   ☐ NO   DATE OF MOST RECENT MARRIAGE   Mo.   Day   Yr

WIDOWED/DIVORCED?   ☐ YES   ☐NO   IF YES, GIVE DATE   Mo.   Day   Ye.

SPOUSE'S FULL BIRTH NAME     SPOUSE'S BIRTHPLACE

**19. IN CASE OF EMERGENCY, NOTIFY** (Person Not Traveling With You)    RELATIONSHIP
(Not Mandatory)
FULL NAME

ADDRESS      (Area Code) PHONE NUMBER

**20. TO BE COMPLETED BY AN APPLICANT WHO BECAME A CITIZEN THROUGH NATURALIZATION**

I IMMIGRATED TO THE U.S.   I RESIDED CONTINUOUSLY IN THE U.S.   DATE NATURALIZED (Mo., Day, Yr.)
(Month, Year)   From (Mo., Yr.)   To (Mo., Yr.)     PLACE

**21. DO NOT SIGN APPLICATION UNTIL REQUESTED TO DO SO BY PERSON ADMINISTERING OATH**

I have not, since acquiring United States citizenship, performed any of the acts listed under "Acts or Conditions" on the reverse of this application form (unless explanatory statemer is attached). I solemnly swear (or affirm) that the statements made on this application are true and the photograph attached is a true likeness of me.

Subscribed and sworn to (affirmed) before me    (SEAL)

Month   Day   Year     X _____

☐ Clerk of Court or
☐ PASSPORT Agent
☐ Postal Employee    (Sign in presence of person authorized to accept application)
☐ (Vice) Consul USA At _____

(Signature of person authorized to accept application)

**22. APPLICANT'S IDENTIFYING DOCUMENTS** ☐ PASSPORT ☐ DRIVER'S LICENSE ☐ OTHER (Specify)    No.

ISSUE DATE   EXPIRATION DATE   PLACE OF ISSUE    ISSUED IN THE NAME OF

Month   Day   Year   Month   Day   Year

**23. FOR ISSUING OFFICE USE ONLY** (Applicant's evidence of citizenship)

☐ Birth Cert.   SR   CR   City   Filed/Issued:    APPLICATION APPROVAL
☐ Passport   Bearer's Name:
☐ Report of Birth    Examiner Name
☐ Naturalization/Citizenship Cert.   No.:
☐ Other:    Office, Date

☐ Seen & Returned    24.

☐ Attached    FEE _____ EXEC _____ POST _____

FORM DSP-11 (12-87)    (SEE INSTRUCTIONS ON REVERSE)    Form Approved OMB No. 1405-0004 (Exp. 8/1/8

Application for a U.S. passport or registration.

# PASSPORT APPLICATION

## FEDERAL TAX LAW:

Section 6039E of the Internal Revenue Code of 1986 requires a passport applicant to provide his/her name (#1), mailing address (#2), date of birth (#5), and social security number (#6). If you have not been issued a social security number, enter zeroes in box #6. Passport Services will provide this information to the Internal Revenue Service routinely. Any applicant who fails to provide the required information is subject to a $500 penalty enforced by the IRS. All questions on this matter should be referred to the nearest IRS office.

## ACTS OR CONDITIONS

(If any of the below-mentioned acts or conditions has been performed by or applies to the applicant, the portion which applies should be lined out, and a supplementary explanatory statement under oath (or affirmation) by the applicant should be attached and made a part of this application.)

I have not, since acquiring United States citizenship, been naturalized as a citizen of a foreign state; taken an oath or made an affirmation or other formal declaration of allegiance to a foreign state; entered or served in the armed forces of a foreign state; accepted or performed the duties of any office, post, or employment under the government of a foreign state or political subdivision thereof; made a formal renunciation of nationality either in the United States or before a diplomatic or consular officer of the United States in a foreign state; or been convicted by a court or court martial of competent jurisdiction of committing any act of treason against, or attempting by force to overthrow, or bearing arms against, the United States, or conspiring to overthrow, put down, or to destroy by force, the Government of the United States; or having been naturalized, within one year after such naturalization, returned to the country of my birth or any other foreign country to take up a permanent residence.

WARNING: False statements made knowingly and willfully in passport applications or in affidavits or other supporting documents submitted therewith are punishable by fine and/or imprisonment under provisions of 18 USC 1001 and/or 18 USC 1542. Alteration or mutilation of a passport issued pursuant to this application is punishable by fine and/or imprisonment under the provisions of 18 USC 1543. The use of a passport in violation of the restrictions contained therein or of the passport regulations is punishable by fine and/or imprisonment under 18 USC 1544. All statements and documents submitted are subject to verification.

## PRIVACY ACT STATEMENT:

The information solicited on this form is authorized by, but not limited to, those statutes codified in Titles 8, 18, and 22, United States Code, and all predecessor statutes whether or not codified, and all regulations issued pursuant to Executive Order 11295 of August 5, 1966. The primary purpose for soliciting the information is to establish citizenship, identity, and entitlement to issuance of a United States Passport or related facility, and to properly administer and enforce the laws pertaining thereto.

The information made available as a routine use on a need-to-know basis to personnel of the Department of State and other government agencies having statutory or other lawful authority to maintain such information in the performance of their official duties, pursuant to a court order; and, as set forth in Part 171, Title 22, Code of Federal Regulations (see Federal Register, Volume 42, pages 49791 through 49795).

Failure to provide the information requested on this form may result in the denial of a United States Passport, related document, or service to the individual seeking such passport, document, or service.

**HOW TO APPLY FOR A U.S. PASSPORT. U.S. passports are issued only to U.S. citizens or nationals.** Each person must obtain his or her own passport.

IF YOU ARE A FIRST-TIME APPLICANT, please complete and submit this application in person. (Applicants under 13 years of age usually need not appear in person unless requested. A parent or guardian may execute the application on the child's behalf.) Each application must be accompanied by (1) PROOF OF U.S. CITIZENSHIP, (2) PROOF OF IDENTITY, (3) TWO PHOTOGRAPHS, (4) FEES (as explained below) to one of the following acceptance agents: a clerk of any Federal or State court of record or a judge or clerk of any probate court accepting applications; a designated postal employee at a selected post office; or an agent at a Passport Agency in Boston, Chicago, Honolulu, Houston, Los Angeles, Miami, New Orleans, New York, Philadelphia, San Francisco, Seattle, Stamford, or Washington, D.C.; or a U.S. consular official.

IF YOU HAVE HAD A PREVIOUS PASSPORT, inquire about eligibility to use Form DSP-82 (mail-in application).

Address requests for passport amendment, extension of validity, or additional visa pages to a Passport Agency or a U.S. Consulate or Embassy abroad. Check visa requirements with consular officials of countries to be visited well in advance of your departure.

(1) PROOF OF U.S. CITIZENSHIP.

(a) APPLICANTS BORN IN THE UNITED STATES. Submit previous U.S. passport or certified birth certificate. A birth certificate must include your given name and surname, date and place of birth, date the birth record was filed, and seal or other certification of the official custodian of such records. A record filed more than 1 year after the birth is acceptable if it is supported by evidence described in the next paragraph.

IF NO BIRTH RECORD EXISTS, submit registrar's notice to that effect. Also submit an early baptismal or circumcision certificate, hospital birth record, early census, school, or family Bible records, newspaper or insurance files, or notarized affidavits of persons having knowledge of your birth (preferably with at least one record listed above). Evidence should include your given name and surname, date and place of birth, and seal or other certification of office (if customary) and signature of issuing official.

(b) APPLICANTS BORN OUTSIDE THE UNITED STATES. Submit previous U.S. passport or Certificate of Naturalization, or Certificate of Citizenship, or a Report of Birth Abroad, or evidence described below.

IF YOU CLAIM CITIZENSHIP THROUGH NATURALIZATION OF PARENT(S), submit the Certificate(s) of Naturalization of your parent(s), your foreign birth certificate, and proof of your admission to the United States for permanent residence.

IF YOU CLAIM CITIZENSHIP THROUGH BIRTH ABROAD TO U.S. CITIZEN PARENT(S), submit a Consular Report of Birth (Form FS-240) or Certification of Birth (Form DS-1350 or FS-545), or your foreign birth certificate, parents' marriage certificate, proof of citizenship of your parent(s), and affidavit of U.S. citizen parent(s) showing all periods and places of residence/physical presence in the United States and abroad before your birth.

(2) PROOF OF IDENTITY. If you are not personally known to the acceptance agent, you must establish your identity to the agent's satisfaction. You may submit items such as the following containing your signature AND physical description or photograph that is a good likeness of you: previous U.S. passport; Certificate of Naturalization or of Citizenship; driver's license (not temporary or learner's license); or government (Federal, State, municipal) identification card or pass. Temporary or altered documents are not acceptable.

IF YOU CANNOT PROVE YOUR IDENTITY as stated above, you must appear with an IDENTIFYING WITNESS who is a U.S. citizen or permanent resident alien who has known you for at least 2 years. Your witness must prove his or her identity and complete and sign an Affidavit of Identifying Witness (Form DSP-71) before the acceptance agent. You must also submit some identification of your own.

(3) TWO PHOTOGRAPHS. Submit two identical photographs of you alone, sufficiently recent to be a good likeness (normally taken within the last 6 months), 2 × 2 inches in size, with an image size from bottom of chin to top of head (including hair) of between 1 and 1-3/8 inches. Photographs must be clear, front view, full face, taken in normal street attire without a hat or dark glasses, and printed on thin paper with a plain light (white or off-white) background. They may be black and white or color. They must be capable of withstanding a mounting temperature of 225° Fahrenheit (107° Celsius). Photographs retouched so that your appearance is changed are unacceptable. Snapshots, most vending machine prints, and magazine or full-length photographs are unacceptable.

(4) FEES. Submit $65 if you are 18 years of age or older. The passport fee is $55. In addition, a fee of $10 is charged for the execution of the application. Your passport will be valid for 10 years from the date of issue except where limited by the Secretary of State to a shorter period. Submit $40 if you are under 18 years of age. The passport fee is $30 and the execution fee is $10. Your passport will be valid for 5 years from the date of issue, except where limited as above.

Pay the passport and execution fees in one of the following forms: check—personal, certified, traveler's, bank draft or cashier's check; money order, U.S. Postal, international, currency exchange; or if abroad, the foreign currency equivalent, or a check drawn on a U.S. bank.

Make passport and execution fees payable to Passport Services (except if applying at a State court, pay execution fee as the State court requires) or the appropriate Embassy or Consulate, if abroad. No fee is charged to applicants with U.S. Government or military authorization for no-fee passports (except State courts may collect the execution fee). Pay special postage if applicable.

LEVELS OF ID    73

# WHAT DO I NEED TO SEND WITH THE APPLICATION FORM?

1. Your most recent passport.
2. A marriage certificate or court order if your name has changed.
3. Passport fee of $55.
4. Two recent (taken within the last 6 months) identical photographs with a light, plain background.

For detailed information on the items to be included, see below.

**1.    YOUR MOST RECENT PASSPORT.**    Issued at age 18 or older in your current name (or see item #2 below) and issued within the past 12 years. If your passport is mutilated or damaged, you must apply on the DSP-11 Application form as specified below.

**2.    A MARRIAGE CERTIFICATE OR COURT ORDER.**    If the name you are currently using differs from the name on your most recent passport, you must submit a marriage certificate or court order showing the change of name. The name change document MUST bear the official seal of the issuing authority. Uncertified copies or notarized documents can not be accepted. All documents will be returned to you with your passport. If you are unable to document your name change in this manner, you must apply on the DSP-11 Application form by making a personal appearance at (1) a passport agency; (2) any Federal or State court of record or any probate court accepting passport applications; or (3) a Post Office which has been selected to accept passport applications.

**3.    THE PASSPORT FEE OF $55.**    Enclose the $55 passport fee in the form of a personal check or money order. DO NOT SEND CASH. Passport services cannot be responsible for cash sent through the mail. If you desire special postage other than first class (registered, special delivery, etc.) include the appropriate fee on the check. THE FULL NAME AND DATE OF BIRTH OF THE APPLICANT MUST BE TYPED OR PRINTED ON THE FRONT OF THE CHECK. MAKE CHECKS PAYABLE TO PASSPORT SERVICES.

**4.    TWO RECENT IDENTICAL PHOTOGRAPHS.**    The photographs must have been taken within the past six months and be a good likeness of you. The photographs must be clear with a full front view of your face and taken on a light (white or off–white) background. Photographs may be in color or black and white and the image size must correspond to the dimensions on the diagram on the front of this form. Photographs must be taken in normal street attire, showing you without headcovering unless a signed statement is submitted indicating that the headcovering is worn daily for religious or medical reasons. Dark glasses may not be worn in passport photographs unless a doctor's statement is submitted supporting the wearing of dark glasses for medical reasons.

| MAIL THIS FORM TO: | DELIVERY – Other Than U.S. Postal Service | FOR INQUIRIES CONTACT: |
|---|---|---|
| National Passport Center<br>P.O. Box 371971<br>Pittsburgh, Pa. 15250–7971 | Mellon Bank<br>Attn: Passport Supervisor, 371971<br>3 Mellon Bank Center, Rm. 153–2723<br>Pittsburgh, Pa. 15259–0001 | National Passport Center<br>31 Rochester Avenue<br>Portsmouth, NH. 03801–2900<br>Telephone: (603) 334–0500 |

## NOTICE TO APPLICANTS RESIDING ABROAD
United States citizens residing abroad CANNOT submit this form to the Passport Facility listed above. Such applicants should contact the nearest United States Embassy or Consulate for procedures to be followed when applying overseas.

## NOTICE TO APPLICANTS FOR OFFICIAL, DIPLOMATIC, OR NO–FEE PASSPORTS
You may use this application if you meet all of the provisions listed above. Submit your U.S. Government or military authorization for a no-fee passport with your application in lieu of the passport fee. CONSULT YOUR SPONSORING AGENCY FOR INSTRUCTIONS ON PROPER ROUTING PROCEDURES BEFORE FORWARDING THIS APPLICATION. Your completed passport will be released to your sponsoring agency for forwarding to you.

## FEDERAL TAX LAW
Section 6039E of the Internal Revenue Code of 1986 requires a passport applicant to provide his/her name, mailing address, date of birth and social security number. If you have not been issued a social security number, enter zeros in box. Passport Services will provide this information to the Internal Revenue Service routinely. Any applicant who fails to provide the required information is subject to a $500 penalty enforced by the IRS. All questions on this matter should be referred to the nearest IRS office.

## PRIVACY ACT STATEMENT
The information solicited on this form is authorized by, but not limited to, those statutes codified in Titles 8, 18, and 22, United States Code, and all predecessor statutes whether or not codified, and all regulations issued pursuant to Executive Order 11295 of August 5, 1966. The primary purpose for soliciting the information is to establish citizenship, identity, and entitlement to issuance of a United States passport or related facility, and to properly administer and enforce the laws pertaining thereto.

The information is made available as a routine use on a need-to-know basis to personnel of the Department of State and of their official duties; pursuant to a court order; and, as set other government agencies having statutory or other lawful authority to maintain such information in the performance of their official duties; pursuant to a court order; and, as set forth in Part 171, Title 22, Code of Federal Regulations (see Federal Register, Volume 42, pages 49791 through 49795).

Failure to provide the information requested on this form may result in the denial of a United States passport, related document, or service to the individual seeking such passport, document, or service.

*Public reporting burden for this collection of information is estimated to average 5 minutes per response, including time required for searching existing data sources, gathering the necessary data, providing the information required, and reviewing the final collection. Send comments on the accuracy of this estimate or the burden and recommendations for reducing it to: Department of State (OIS/RA/DIR) Washington, D.C. 20520–0284, and to the Office of Information and Regulatory Affairs, Office of Management and Budget, Paperwork Reduction Project (1405–0020), Washington, D.C. 20503.

UNITED STATES DEPARTMENT OF STATE

# APPLICATION FOR PASSPORT BY MAIL

TYPE OR PRINT IN INK IN WHITE AREAS ONLY          USE BLOCK LETTERS/NUMBERS

| NAME | FIRST | | MIDDLE | |
|------|-------|--|--------|--|

| LAST | |
|------|--|

MAIL PASSPORT TO

| STREET / RFD # OR P.O. BOX | | APT. # |
|----------------------------|--|--------|

| CITY | STATE | ZIP CODE |
|------|-------|----------|

IN CARE OF (IF APPLICABLE)

R    D    O    DP    Issue Date _____

End.# _____          Exp. _____

| SEX □ Male □ Female | PLACE OF BIRTH City & State or City & Country | | DATE OF BIRTH  Month  Day  Year | SOCIAL SECURITY NUMBER (SEE FEDERAL TAX LAW NOTICE ON REVERSE SIDE) |
|---------------------|----------------------------------------------|--|----------------------------------|---------------------------------------------------------------------|

| HEIGHT Feet Inches | HAIR COLOR | EYE COLOR | HOME TELEPHONE ( ) | BUSINESS TELEPHONE ( ) |
|--------------------|------------|-----------|--------------------|------------------------|

**NOTE: Most recent passport MUST be enclosed!**

| PASSPORT NUMBER | ISSUE DATE  Month  Day  Year | PLACE OF ISSUANCE | OCCUPATION (Not Mandatory) |
|-----------------|------------------------------|-------------------|----------------------------|

| DEPARTURE DATE | TRAVEL PLANS (Not Mandatory) COUNTRIES TO BE VISITED | LENGTH OF STAY (Not Mandatory) |
|----------------|-----------------------------------------------------|--------------------------------|

| PERMANENT ADDRESS (Do not list P.O. Box) STREET / R.F.D. # | CITY | STATE | ZIP CODE |
|-----------------------------------------------------------|------|-------|----------|

NOT MANDATORY

IN CASE OF EMERGENCY WHEN TRAVELING ABROAD, NOTIFY (Person In U.S. Not Traveling With You)

| NAME | |
|------|--|

| STREET | |
|--------|--|

| CITY | STATE | ZIP CODE |
|------|-------|----------|

| TELEPHONE ( ) | RELATIONSHIP |
|---------------|--------------|

FROM 1" TO 1-3/8"

2" X 2"

SUBMIT TWO RECENT IDENTICAL PHOTOS WITH LIGHT PLAIN BACKGROUND

**OATH AND SIGNATURE** (If any of the below-mentioned acts or conditions have been performed by or apply to the applicant the portion which applies should be lined out, and a supplementary explanatory statement should be attached, signed, and made a part of this application.)

I have not, since acquiring United States citizenship, been naturalized as a citizen of a foreign state; taken any oath, or made an affirmation or other formal declaration of allegiance to a foreign state; entered or served in the armed forces of a foreign state; accepted or performed the duties of any office, post, or employment under the Government of a foreign state or political subdivision thereof; made a formal renunciation of nationality either in the United States or before a diplomatic or consular officer of the United States in a foreign state; or been convicted by a court or court martial of competent jurisdiction of committing any act of treason against, or attempting by force to overthrow, or bearing arms against the United States, or conspiring to overthrow, put down or destroy by force the Government of the United States.

WARNING: False statements made knowingly and willfully in passport applications or affidavits or other supporting documents are punishable by fine and imprisonment under the provisions of 18 USC 1001 and/or 18 USC 1542. The alteration or mutilation of a passport issued pursuant to this application is punishable by fine and/or imprisonment under 18 USC 1543. The use of a passport in violation of the restrictions therein is punishable by fine and/or imprisonment under 18 USC 1544.

DECLARATION: I declare that the statements made in this application are true and complete to the best of my knowledge and belief, that the attached photograph are a true likeness of me, and that I have not been issued or included in a passport issued subsequent to the one submitted herein.

**NOTE: APPLICANT MUST SIGN & DATE**

| SIGNATURE | | DATE |
|-----------|--|------|

DO NOT WRITE BELOW THIS SPACE  – FOR PASSPORT SERVICES USE ONLY –  DO NOT WRITE BELOW THIS SPACE

| Application Approval | Evidence of Name Change □ Marriage Cert.  □ Court Order  Date _____  Place _____  From _____  To _____ | Fees |
|----------------------|--------------------------------------------------------------------------------------------------------------|------|

FORM DSP-82 (2-93)                    OMB No. 1405-0020 (Exp. 7/31/93) Estimated Burden - 5 Minutes

LEVELS OF ID          75

## APPLICATION FOR MAILBOX RENTAL

This Agreement made ____/____/____ by and between _____

of _____, hereinafter referred to as "Applicant" and

_____ 's hereinafter referred to as ... ', shall be governed by these terms to which

each party agrees:

1. By completing this form and USPS Form 1583, a copy of which will be made available to the United States Postal Service, applicant appoints : s as agent for the receipt of mail for a period not to exceed that for which rent has been paid in advance. : will provide a key to a lockbox from which applicant may obtain his or her mail. Access to applicant's lockbox will be provided during the business hours posted by : . Should applicant appoint another person or organization to collect mail from : . premises, applicant shall be responsible for the conduct of such person or organization. shall assume that possession of a key is evidence of authority to collect mail.

2. The key loaned to applicant remains the property of and shall not be duplicated or modified by applicant. Applicant shall be refunded the key deposit upon return of the key, within ten (10) days of termination of service.

3. Applicant understands that the relationship of the parties hereto is one of bailment and not landlord and tenant.

4. Once . : : has placed applicant's mail in the assigned lockbox, the mail shall be deemed to have been delivered to applicant, and .. : shall not be responsible for loss, theft or damage thereto. : . is not engaged in the delivery of mail and cannot be responsible for failure of the United States Postal Service to deliver mail or to deliver it in a timely fashion or undamaged condition.

5. Applicant agrees to us :..... services in accordance with these rules and in compliance with U.S. Postal regulations, as well as local, state and federal statutes and regulations. Failure to do so may result in cancellation of service without notice.

6. All information provided by applicant on this form is confidential and will not knowingly be disclosed to anyone without applicant's prior consent, except for law enforcement purposes.

7. Mail will not be accepted for more than three (3) persons or organizations in a single lockbox. In the event that applicant consistently receives substantially more mail than can be placed in a single lockbox, . ' reserves the right to require applicant to rent additional boxes.

8. Applicant agrees to protect, indemnify and hold harmless : , from and against any and all claims, demands and causes of action of any nature whatsoever relative to use of ' , facilities or services, and any expense of incurred in a defense against same shall be reimbursed by applicant.

9. In the event . ' : ' commits or fails to commit any act which results in disruption of service to applicant, and applicant thereby suffers a loss, i :...... liability shall be limited to not more than the rental fees paid by applicant for service not yet received.

10. Certified, registered, insured or C.O.D. mail or parcels will not be accepted by . as an agent for applicant.

11. : fees are due and payable in advance. Failure to pay such fees when due may result in disruption or cancellation of services. does not prorate its fees and does not provide refunds in the event applicant cancels service prior to its agreed upon expiration.

12. The address to be used by applicant is as follows:

Your Name
: . Blaine Dept. _____
Moscow, ID 83843

13. Applicant shall not use the designation "Box" as part of his/her address, but may use "Dept.". Applicant is responsible for notifying correspondence of the above address.

14. Upon termination of services by .. : or failure to pay rent in advance by applicant, ' :... shall be responsible for holding applicant's mail for up to thirty (30) days during which time applicant may retrieve said mail. After this retrieval of mail, ! : shall refuse to accept further mail for applicant, shall mark all such mail "No longer at this address. Return to sender," and redeposit such mail into the U.S. Postal System. After service is discontinued or canceled : .. shall not forward mail to applicant unless applicant requests this service in advance and has made arrangements to pay for such service, including the postage required.

_____        _____
Agent                                                      Customer

_____
Co-worker

A sample application for commercial mailbox rental.

**(Item 2 for P.O. Use ONLY)**

| | |
|---|---|
| 1. Name to which box number(s) is (are) assigned | 2. Box/Caller Nos. _____ Thru _____ |

3. Name of person making application *(If representing an organization, show title and name of organization if different from above)*

4. Will this box be used for soliciting or doing business with the public? *(Check one)*
   a. ☐ Yes   b. ☐ No

| | |
|---|---|
| 5. Address *(No., Street, City, State and ZIP Code. Record address change on reverse and line out address below.)* | 6. Telephone No. *(If any)* |

**APPLICANT PLEASE NOTE:** Execution of this application signifies your agreement to comply with all postal rules relative to post office boxes and caller service.

| | |
|---|---|
| 7. Signature of applicant *(Same as Item 3)* | 8. Date of application |

**ITEMS 8-14: TO BE COMPLETED BY POST OFFICE**

| 9. Type of identification *(Driver's license, military identification, other; show identification no.)* | 10. Eligibility for carrier-delivery ☐ CITY ☐ RURAL ☐ NONE | 11. Box size needed |
|---|---|---|

| 12. Dates of Service | | 13. Service Assigned | 14. Information Verified by |
|---|---|---|---|
| a. Started | b. Ended | a. ☐ Post Office Box   b. ☐ Caller   c. ☐ Reserve Number | a. *(Initials)* |

**PS Form 1093,** June 1993 — **(PART I) APPLICATION FOR POST OFFICE BOX OR CALLER SERVICE**

| SPECIAL ORDERS | ITEMS 16-18: TO BE COMPLETED BY POST OFFICE |
|---|---|
| 15. Postmaster: The following persons, or authorized representatives of the organizations listed are authorized to accept mail addressed to this (these) post office box or caller number(s). Continue on reverse if necessary. ☒ Check if reverse is used. | 16. Post Office Box/Caller number for which this card is applicable _____ through _____ |
| a. Applicant *(Same as Item 3)* | 17. ☐ Check if box is to be used for Express Mail reshipment. |
| b. Name of box customer *(Same as Item 1)* | 18. Post Office Date Stamp |
| c. Other | |
| d. Other | |
| CUSTOMER NOTE: Possession of post office box key or combination may be considered by the Postal Service to be valid evidence that possessor is authorized to remove mail from boxes. | 19. I have read instructions and will comply |
| | Signature of Applicant *(Same as Item 3)* |

**PS Form 1093,** June 1993 — **(PART II) APPLICATION FOR POST OFFICE BOX OR CALLER SERVICE**

Application for U.S. Post Office mailbox rental.

### INSTRUCTIONS FOR WORKING COMBINATION BOX

1. Clear dial by three revolutions to the right, stop on _____
2. Turn dial to the left and stop the second time around on _____
3. Turn right and stop at _____
4. Turn latch key LEFT to open.

Your ZIP + 4 is: [ ][ ][ ][ ][ ] — [ ][ ][ ][ ]

## Rules for use of Post Office Box and Caller Service

IMPORTANT: Post Office Box and Caller Service are Subject to the following and the regulations in Parts 951 and 952 DMM.

I. Mail, which is properly addressed to a post office box or caller service number, will be delivered through that post office box or caller service.

II. Customers must promptly notify correspondents of their current box or caller number address.

III. Post office box or caller service fees are paid in advance for one or two semiannual periods. A notice of fees due will be placed in a box or included with caller mail 20 days before the due date. If a boxholder is out of town and has submitted a temporary forwarding order, the notice will be mailed to the temporary address. It is the responsibility of the boxholder to assure that payment is made on time. If payment is sent by mail, it must be received by the postmaster by the due date. Payment may be by cash, or by check payable to the postmaster. Do not send cash by mail. If a check is returned by the bank, the box will be closed until that check is made good.

IV. If fee is not paid on time, the post office box will be secured so that mail cannot be removed through the door. If box or caller fees are not paid after 10 days, mail will be removed and treated as undeliverable, unless it can be forwarded in accordance with a change of address order. Closed post office boxes will be immediately available to new customers.

V. Post office boxes or caller service may not be used for any purpose prohibited by postal regulations. See Domestic Mail Manual, (DMM).

VI. Boxes and caller numbers may not be used for the sole purpose of having the Postal Service forward or transfer mail to another address free of charge.

VII. Boxholders must promptly remove mail, or have it removed, from their boxes. Advance arrangements must be specifically made with the postmaster if mail is to be accumulated for more than 30 days and an overflow condition is probable.

VIII. Keys for key-type post office boxes will be issued upon payment of $1 for each key, including those initially issued for each post office box. When a box is surrendered, all keys must be returned to the Postal Service. Fees for up to 2 keys will be returned to the boxholder. Keys for post office boxes may be obtained only from the Postal Service.

IX. Customers who use post office box or caller service, are required to maintain a current Form 1093, Application for Post Office Box or Caller Service, on file with the Postal Service. Any information on the application, which changes or becomes obsolete, must be corrected by promptly updating the Form 1093 on file with the postmaster at the office where the post office box or caller service is used.

X. Box or caller service may be terminated as provided in the DMM.

The customer may appeal a termination of service in writing to higher authority by following the detailed procedures in the DMM.

XI. Concerning information required for the completion of this form:

A. The collection of this information is authorized by 39 U.S.C. 403,404.

B. This information will be used to provide the applicant with post office box or caller service.

C. This information may be routinely disclosed:

1. To persons authorized by law to serve judicial process for the purpose of serving such process.

2. To a government agency, when necessary for the performance of its duties.

3. To anyone, when the box is being used for the purpose of doing or soliciting business to the public.

4. To a Congressional Office, at the request of the boxholder.

5. In response to a subpoena or court order.

6. Where pertinent to a legal proceeding in which the Postal Service is a party.

D. Completion of this form is voluntary; however, if this information is not provided, the applicant will be unable to use a box or receive caller service.

XII. Refer to the DMM for a more detailed explanation of these regulations.

PS Form 1093, June 1993 (PART III)

# 6

# HOMEMADE STATE & PROVINCIAL DRIVER'S LICENSES

First it is vital to decide exactly why a new driver's license is necessary. As previously mentioned, although new driver's licenses are ridiculously easy to home-manufacture using modern electronic equipment, vital numbers not accurately contained in a forgery will immediately tip off any official able and inclined to check central records. This includes most (but not all) traffic stops, precluding one from using a homemade driver's license, in many instances, as an actual license to drive.

In times past, long-haul commercial truckers were notorious for the large number of different legal state licenses they acquired and carried. It was an easy matter, they admit, to take two or three easily acquired level two and three IDs and a well-rehearsed cock-and-bull story to state licensing offices, where they were issued license after license in their own and whatever fictitious names they desired. Some admit to having had as many as four or five different licenses, often from as many different states.

The National Commercial Motor Vehicle Safety Act of 1986 stopped much of that. This act mandated that all states issue and enforce a national commercial motor vehicle license called a commercial driver's license (CDL). Additionally, it linked all state licenses in one giant computerized system "to share information." These include Class-D or private driver's licenses as well. At least eight different driving infractions are also cataloged in the computer data base. Any convictions, suspensions, revocations, or cancellations are duly noted on the offending driver's record.

A new IDer will probably not wish to get a national CDL. If he does, he must turn in his valid Class-D license (private vehicle) and take a written test. Outright counterfeiting of these CDLs is not difficult using a computer system, but if one of them is checked, the subterfuge will be uncovered immediately. Your number will be cross-checked if you are stopped while carrying one of these cards.

Securing multiple legal state licenses is not tough if you can make use of such. All it takes is a valid Social Security number attached to another alias and a good pretext for why at age 47 you are getting your first driver's license. Clerks at license bureaus are obviously nervous about the process, but it has worked recently in two different states for people to claim that they have been in Canada the last eight years and now need a U.S. driver's license again. You can acquire as many different state licenses as you have different Social Security numbers.

If a clerk asks for a birth certificate rather than a Social Security card, so much the better. Even modestly good computer-generated birth certificates work. Driver's license people have hardly a clue about how to qualify a genuine birth certificate. In states that do not require Social Security numbers, this ploy is very simple.

Don't claim that your license was lost or stolen. Clerks at the license bureau can look it up for you on their computer. Applicants with valid Social Security numbers can simply say they never had a state license. Officials will search their computer for your Social Security number and name, grumble a lot when they can't find a record of a past license, and then issue the license.

Other than presentation during traffic-related matters, the second most common use of a driver's license is as backup ID when paying by check or credit card. Demonstrating proof of age in bars is the third most frequent use of driver's licenses, experts claim. For many of us, having to prove age is in the distant past.

Getting caught with an obviously copied or otherwise altered driver's license at a bar is a frequent occurrence. Door checkers at places likely to be frequented by illegal minors are stringently cautious. It does not hurt a bar's business to reject an occasional document that seems "off color," whereas passing even one underage imbiber into an inner sanctum can have serious repercussions.

Reports from various university campuses suggest that production of counterfeit driver's licenses has become big business for some entrepreneurs. In that regard, a serious new IDer might find productive employment for his computer gear even before disappearing.

Floyd, our new IDer, desperately wanted some kind of new ID driver's license to use when he first left his old digs. Unfortunately, at that time he did not know how to produce a new license or where he could purchase one. Computer technology has only recently evolved to the point where manufacture or purchase is a serious consideration. But what a difference a year makes! In many large cities, especially in the south and west, it is now possible to purchase excellent, ready-made fake driver's licenses perfect for everything except driving (if you are checked by the police). In San Francisco and Orange Counties, California, counterfeiters openly advertise in underground publications—if that isn't a contradiction in terms. The equipment used is similar to that in state license bureaus.

Floyd resolved to drive with extreme caution—not too fast, too slow, or too erratically. He wanted an alternative license in the event he was involved in a routine traffic stop or was a witness to another accident or fender bender.

Traffic police claim that they call in license numbers for verification only about half the time they check licenses. Because he could not display his old license and still remain in hiding, he was essentially driving to his new location without a driver's license. His plan, if he got into anything that required him to show a driver's license, was to claim he left his license at home and try to talk his way out of the situation. Fortunately, this was not necessary.

As an aside, ID checkers at bars, banks, and even official places such as police roadblocks, claim that most forgeries and tampered documents are easily spotted.

"In many cases, new users can't even recite back their own (but forged) name and address," Maud Merica, an old cathouse owner, who now runs a respectable beer hall for college kids, told me. "Frayed edges of the plastic laminate and/or obvious picture tampering are dead giveaways. We check for obvious odd-looking or tampered-with documents, but when we find them we seldom take action. I can't recall ever calling numbers in for verification," she concluded.

In that regard, Maud is right on the money. Generally, people look for obviously altered real IDs, with little thought given to complete forgeries. I asked Maud about good forgeries.

"I don't really know of any," she said. "Some of the documents we look at are really scuffed and beaten up as a result of general wear. We always pass these on through without much comment."

In this admission lies great promise. The fact that rough, well-worn documents are usually accepted suggests that you should age any newly manufactured driver's license by running it through several washer-dryer cycles or working it over with very fine steel wool.

For whatever reason, those requiring a genuine-looking driver's license absolutely must secure a copy of the *current* full-color publication, *I.D. Checking Guide*. This nifty 96-page book is published by the Driver's License Guide Company, Box 5303, Redwood City, CA 94063. It costs about $23, including postage. But money, in this case, is not the obstacle.

Driver's License Guide Company officially puts prospective buyers of its book through a little song-and-dance routine intended to weed out the "unworthy." This makes acquisition difficult but certainly not impossible. The company will *not* sell to authors, private investigators, or consultants, much less regular, law-abiding citizens or—heaven forbid!—forgers. It markets the booklet to law enforcement agencies and enterprises that legally have to check IDs before selling certain items (e.g., bars and liquor stores).

The book contains good but, in some cases not scannable, color reproductions of driver's licenses for all 50 states, the Canadian provinces, and Puerto Rico. Also included are examples of INS documents, U.S. State Department driver's licenses, and even military IDs.

All the information in this booklet is extremely valuable in terms of knowing the latest license formats, correct colors, use of holograms, and camera numbers, and—most of all—for understanding which state licenses are easiest to reproduce. Unfortunately, the material does not contain information regarding what, if any, copy is on the reverse of the card or to what extent official holograms disappear from view as the card is carried and used.

Some of our nation's libraries carry copies of the *I.D. Checking Guide* in their reference section. Many university libraries also have copies that cannot be taken out (for possible use in a scanner). The publisher will sell to

Production of driver's licenses is not difficult, especially if you have a current copy of *I.D. Checking Guide*.

educational institutions; a high school teacher ordered the copies now lying in front of me.

The people at Driver's License Guide Company claim that if someone unfamiliar orders a copy of the booklet on letterhead reading Pete's Bar and Grill, they will call the listed number to be sure that Pete really is checking IDs at the door of the bar to be sure that no underage drinkers are admitted.

Producing Pete's Bar and Grill letterhead on a computer is a piece of cake. No one I know of has received a verifying call as yet, but undoubtedly this will change when this book hits the market. Be prepared to stand by your phone with a "Hello, this is Pete's" response.

Although it is basically true that it is cleaner and easier to work with a valid driver's license for the state in which you want a new ID, pictures in the *I.D. Checking Guide* are still helpful. In many cases, the publishers have used graphic-enhancement techniques to better reproduce otherwise difficult-to-see validation seals and holograms. These examples can be scanned into a computer and, using Photoshop, moved around to augment the faded, incomplete image taken from an actual driver's license.

Again using Photoshop, enlarge, and enhance weak portions of the copy. Lift the old text copy from the license and insert the new information of your choosing.

The first time I made up a new driver's license from scratch, it took about five hours. The results were very good, and the color was perfect. But part of this production cycle included learning how to use an edit program and getting a good scan on the license I had to work with. Currently, it takes about one hour to scan in, edit, and print out a new driver's license, assuming you already have the appropriate picture in hand.

My color ink-jet printer works fine, provided that I go to an actual photo shop for color pictures needed as part of the license. Original license colors in these cases are all very basic. An average color printer (not a color laser printer) handles the work nicely.

Until relatively recently Canadian licenses did not include pictures, but this is changing. Some are no more than typed documents on etched paper and are so easy to copy that it is ridiculous. Perhaps this explains why Canadian authorities are in such a heat to change to photo licenses.

Initially, some problems came up when I tried to laminate a reproduction license. I quickly found that it was not wise to take a newly minted driver's license to local stationery shops for lamination. One clerk was in turn puzzled, surprised, and infuriated at my request to laminate a license that he could not tell from an original. Instead, I purchased a hot-roller laminating machine along with an ample supply of clear plastic material.

Probably the greatest challenge to this entire process involves securing representative samples of various state driver's licenses to scan into the computer. This is especially true if the state in which you wish to secure a new license is far away from your current residence. Even if you live in the state in which you wish to replicate a license, it will hardly work to walk up to someone and ask to scan his driver's license. Securing sample licenses, other than your own, is a far greater problem than you would initially suppose.

Also, it is a good, basic rule of thumb in this business that the best, simplest licenses that would work ideally for your specific new ID program are always found in states at least 500 miles away from your current residence. At any rate, producing your own driver's licenses at home is not much of a problem once you think your way into the system, deciding that's what you really need and want.

# 7

# HOMEMADE INTERNATIONAL DRIVER'S LICENSE

Opinions differ widely about the practical value of an international driver's license. As a result, or perhaps out of fundamental ignorance, most new ID advocates spend little or no time discussing it. At worst, an international driver's license is a good supporting document. At best, it becomes a stand-alone photo ID, useful for everything from being an ersatz driver's license to cash checks, establish a mail box ID, or even open a bank account.

As a level-two picture ID, an international driver's license is ideal. It does not include a Social Security number, and verification is virtually impossible, especially

An international driver's license is not a level-one identity document, but it has been used in some very unusual circumstances as that very thing. You can easily counterfeit one by using only a photocopier and colored pencils.

on short notice. Use them in conjunction with other level-three ID, such as the front page of a tax return, library card, or even a simple business card. Home manufacture on even the most basic office machines is ridiculously easy. Computer desktop publishing systems can make the process quicker and easier, but is *not* essential.

The greatest risk involves the fact that issuers may tighten up their procedures, making this information obsolete very soon after publication of this book.

Standard international driver's licenses are issued by any one of the more than 1,000 American Automobile Association (AAA, pronounced and sometimes written as Triple A) offices located throughout the United States. The cost is $10 if two-color, passport-sized photos are supplied or $15.25 if AAA takes the Polaroids. All that is needed to secure the document other than $15.25 cash is a current driver's license. Theoretically, it would be easy to secure an international license by using a computer-generated driver's license complete with your new name. No cross-checks are made by the issuer to determine whether the document is valid. But this procedure involves more middlemen or women than are necessary. Start your career as a new ID document manufacturer by producing your very own international driver's license.

Begin by going to a local AAA office to purchase a legitimate international driver's license, using your current state license as a validating document. Including picture taking, the process consumes at most a quarter of an hour. Walk away with a little, gray-cardboard-covered 4 1/2-x-6-inch booklet with instructions printed in eight different languages. The name and address are filled out in pen on the last page near where the color passport photo is glued (not laminated). In the past some photos were stapled to the booklet.

Three very simple, easily copied red AAA stamps placed around the picture validate the document. A stamp is also placed next to the category of vehicles the carrier is legally allowed to operate. Standard red art pencils can be employed to make these marks at home. There is nothing intricate or different about the stamp design. Receipts issued by AAA at the time the original license is purchased have logos that provide an ideal pattern for reproduction.

A serial number on the front cover will eventually lead to the issuing office. Alter these numbers in the computer, or if you are using a photocopier to make your license, simply leave them as they are. If tracking could be a genuine problem, secure a sample international driver's permit by using a bogus homemade state license. A second picture and extremely simple application are filled out at the local issuing AAA office (in the case of genuine documents). These documents are supposedly filed at local AAA offices forever.

Those seeking very deep cover should travel several hundred miles to get their first model international permit from which all others are made. Many new IDers will probably manufacture two or three of these little beauties.

Cover stock used to manufacture the 13-page booklets has varied over the years. Currently, most seem to be constructed from paper known as Wasau Royal Fiber Cover Sheet Recycled Pewter, available at virtually all full-service stationery stores. Inside sheets are standard gray mimeo paper. The cost per sheet is nominal. If this is your first homemade document, purchase several sheets of paper on which to practice.

Disassemble the booklet and run the various pages front and back through a copy machine. Lining up everything front and back is a challenge. Simpler personal copiers are probably easier to use. Bigger automated copy machines often are difficult in terms of knowing which way to orient the paper and getting front and back collated.

Using a table-type paper cutter, not scissors, trim out the pages. Staple the internal pages together, collating them per the original. On the front cover is a line on which to fill in the first date this permit is valid. AAA allows holders to date anytime ahead, up to one year, coinciding with the planned international departure. Dates on your home-grown document can be filled in, appropriately documenting a return from overseas, likely departure, or whatever you wish.

Practice producing red AAA seals on a similar sheet of paper before attempting an assembled booklet. Start by tracing around the stock logo from AAA's receipt. Lay out the AAAs with a ruler and then fill in the little oval with red pencil. Nobody will look very closely, but you should still do a nice, neat job. The color may not be exact, but, again, no one will know. Different offices issue many tiny variations of this same document. I have four original international driving permits, all of which are slightly different.

Name, address, and other data are filled in on the last page on lines one through five. Pictures used are about 2-x-2-inch, passport-sized. The policy now is to use color. Total time, start to finish, including going to AAA for the original sample and scrounging up paper stock, is less than eight hours. Copy work time in local office support store such as Kinko's or Office Mate seems to be the bulk of the project.

According to a local bank customer service representative, banks sometimes open checking accounts for students using international driver's licenses who also have some other form of secondary ID. Traffic cops claim they generally do *not* take an international driver's license for ID because there is absolutely no legal basis for doing so. As a practical matter, they often accept them for such minor infractions as broken taillights, improper parking violations, or routine stops, if there is no moving violation or indication of drunk driving.

Because foreign national driver's licenses are obscure and difficult to find as working examples, they are difficult to duplicate. But anyone who can find a license to copy, particularly from Central and South America or Asia, will have little difficulty using basically the same procedure as for international licenses. My good friend Maurice drove for eight months in the United States on a Thai license. Whenever he was checked, the officer had to ask him if this was a valid license. U.S. traffic cops do not usually read Thai. Eventually, Maurice traded the document in for a Maryland license without having to take a test on anything. He was asked a few questions about what he was doing overseas and where he was living, and that was it. This device works best wherever a large number of foreigners and travelers are found. License bureaus where there are universities, world corporate headquarters of large international companies, and immigrant congregation points are excellent places in which to trade homemade foreign driver's licenses for state licenses.

Thai driver's licenses are made on the commonest of gray paper stock. European driver's licenses are usually laminated in plastic. They are easily made on one's computer, but not by using a simple Xerox and colored pencils, as are some Asian and South American licenses.

International driver's licenses have worked as IDs to place ads (obituaries) in local papers, to secure library cards, and to rent mail boxes, both public and private. They will also work nicely as check-cashing IDs in many, many places.

Only real driver's licenses are better. These are harder to produce, but certainly not impossible, given modern technology.

# 8

# UNUSUAL ID AND ITS EMPLOYMENT

"I just hate it when students bring in weird identification that we have never seen before, expecting us to take immediate action," a frustrated clerk at the employment office of a state university recently complained.

"We have no real way of judging the authenticity of these materials," she continued, "especially when they hit us with them out of the clear blue. In many cases, it looks like we are displaying some sort of prejudice if we even question them.

"Seems like it is almost always the Native Americans or the Afro-Americans who use this stuff," she went on in exasperation. "These people seem to have a strange desire to use something peculiar or out of the ordinary. Sometimes this precludes us from engaging in a normal conversation. When I don't immediately approve the strange documents they display, I am accused of being a racist. I could even lose my job over what is something pretty insignificant. It has never happened yet, but I could easily approve the wrong—or maybe a fictitious—document, getting the university in big trouble with the INS, the student loan office, or whatever. It's a no-win situation for me; I never really know what to do," she concluded.

Though it is way beyond the scope and purpose of this book to solve problems of university employment offices, the lesson to those who are thinking about new ID should be obvious. This clerk's frustration points up the ease with which obscure identification documents can be made up and deployed against those who seldom or never have previously seen such. You only need some documents from which to model and a great deal of belligerent brass when presenting them.

Who, for instance, has ever even seen a U.S. Coast Guard Merchant Mariner card or a Native American tribal document? There are even Basque identification cards floating around. Basques look like any other Europeans.

Tribal documents can and do exist in dozens of totally different forms and patterns ranging from the ultrasimple to extremely gaudy. All I have seen are easily reproduced on color scanners and printers. Some do not even include pictures, creating a situation where they may not even be legal IDs.

In one case, rather than convincing a visiting chief that his documentation was improper, the clerk inserted a color picture in a document that normally did not include one. Many of these documents are simple enough to accommodate this sort of manipulation.

Mina Brookie was one-eighth Miami Indian. She lived in north-central Indiana, and she looked about like any one of the folks who stepped ashore at Plymouth Rock. She greatly enjoyed flashing around her tribal card to which her one-eighth Miami lineage entitled her, even before we were conditioned to treat such things with great respect. Copies of her tribal card are now a permanent part of my ID document collection.

Should it ever become necessary to deal with an especially obstinate government bureaucracy, many of which are already paranoid about minorities, I will call the document up on the computer; take out the original owner's name, address, and date; and insert a new name, address, and picture for the circumstances. After lamination I am an instant Native American, gray hair and all. Using a bit of creativity, I could acquire a title and tribal office with all the rights and privileges attached.

Most people will take a certificate of U.S. citizenship or naturalization for both identity and employment eligibility. My father's original documents dating from the mid-1920s are neither complex nor difficult to duplicate using a computer. I haven't seen a great many other of these documents and doubt whether bank officers, driver's license bureau clerks, or Social Security office clerks have either.

One can safely assume that hundreds or maybe even thousands of different forms exist. My guess is that the INS itself would have problems sorting home-manufactured documents from the real documents that have been issued through the years.

Of course, smart new IDers won't present newly manufactured documents to agencies that could be firsthand evaluators of their own document issues. However, when used to authenticate and support claims to insurance companies, travel agents, medical providers, newspaper reporters, or loan officers, these documents can be quite good.

Most counties will happily give you a copy of your own voter registration card. Basically these are similar from state to state and identical within a state. Some are so simple they can be made up on a Xerox. Others require a computer and scanner. Often, county clerks simply hand out the blank cards with the instruction to "fill this out." I told a country clerk I was moving and needed the card for voter identification at my new location. When the clerk gave me a blank card, I simply walked out with my old card and a new blank one. In this case I didn't even have to produce a new card on my scanner.

Stamps used to validate these documents are simple and, in many cases, worn, illegible affairs that are easily duplicated by using stamps from one of the mail-order supply houses. Like so much of our documentation, people 100 miles away have no idea exactly what the correct form is. A relative of new IDer Ken claims to have secured a real U.S. passport by using an American Indian ID card and a voter registration card. He says he appeared in person at the Seattle office and put up a belligerent front before the passport clerk.

If used around military bases, homemade "official military dependent cards" are of dubious value. Too many people know exactly what they should look like, unless you can find a clerk too bored to give the document more than a passing glance. Generally, dependent military IDs are consistent throughout the world; everybody used to taking them knows what they are supposed to look like. In other places few, if any, citizens have ever seen one of these. Under these circumstances, well-done computer-generated versions work wonderfully.

By using a computer, scanner, and color printer, new dependent cards can be made that defy detection. This is a good example of a document that must be made perfectly or not at all. The trick to making them well involves having a working Social Security number to use on the reproduction. An agency that cross-checks by Social Security number will come up with a blank, placing the user at great peril.

Many Third World foreign passports are ridiculously easy to duplicate, if you can secure an example from which to work. Some are so simple, being made of heavy, off-color paper, that they can be run off on a copy machine, much like the process for manufacturing international driver's licenses. More important, few people are going to know what a genuine Kenyan, Indonesian, or Jordanian passport is supposed to look like. A check at the appropriate embassy will expose a forgery, but hope that your situation will not attract enough interest to warrant such heavy-duty investigation. A retired State Department employee confirms that in the Washington, D.C., area and near many large universities, foreign nationals frequently acquire U.S. driver's licenses without Social Security numbers by using foreign passports and visas. Most driver's license clerks do not know what language somebody from Surinam, for instance, should speak, nor what coloring and personal features are appropriate. You will have to take a driving and language test, which is, of course, no hurdle after presenting your foreign passport as proof of identity.

Although parlaying a counterfeit foreign passport into all sorts of good documents is relatively easy, the drawback to this scheme is that it is often desperately difficult to find originals from which to work. An enterprising university student in the east tried to supplement his income by purchasing the right to scan foreign students' passports and other documents issued by the U.S. government to them into his computer. Unfortunately, not enough people with whom he associated were interested in purchasing his stock documents. After a year or so, the project went toes up. Today, the fellow has quite a nice collection of foreign passports and immigration documents, but no plans to become a new IDer or otherwise use this treasure trove.

Some of the other documents he has on his computer range from unique to obscure. These include samples of alien registration cards, temporary resident cards, employment authorization cards, reentry permits, refugee travel documents, and employment authorization cards. He also has a listing of color and weight of paper used on originals; listing is done by American stock number. His inventory of passports is similarly cataloged.

Some of these originals are complex, and some have stamps used only on those specific documents that would be foolishly risky to have duplicated. But all of these documents, including stamp, are reproducible on a modern color scanner and printer.

I asked this student about the general utility of these documents. His response was classical new ID, although the fellow himself is not a new IDer.

"Most normal people," he replied, "have never heard of most of these document, much less examined them. Under recent INS regulations, some employers are becoming knowledgeable about what is legal and what it should look like. But in most cases this is not true. In some places, however, manufacture of documents for illegal workers has become widespread. Expect documents to be closely examined wherever this type forgery has been uncovered or is widely practiced.

"If I use one of these papers to rent an apartment or buy a car, nobody will ever know they were made up the day before in my office," he chuckles.

This fellow also believes he could use a homemade foreign birth certificate and a naturalization certificate to acquire a new ID Social Security number for a person over 25 years of age. Someone affecting a credible foreign accent might pull it off, but there is no current success story to verify it.

The device is probably no riskier than going into a Social Security office with a friend who claims you are someone "developmentally challenged who is now being mainstreamed back into society." Some writers also claim that older new IDers have successfully applied for Social Security cards by claiming that they were members of a cloistered religious sect. This sounds good, except I am sure that Social Security administrators read new ID books. No doubt, several memos have been circulated warning bureaucrats to be on the alert for such a pretext.

Most Asian, African, and South or Central American driver's licenses are extremely easy to manufacture at home. All are produced on the commonest of paper, and some don't even have pictures. A man from Turkey who lived in our community even used a Turkish bicycle license as a form of identification. U.S. officials would probably have an easier time believing I was a Turk than believing that any country actually issues national bicycle licenses, had I decided to make and use such a document. Yet, if they can be deployed productively, these sorts of licenses can be made from scratch because no one is going to know how they are supposed to look. Samples of the written language to be used can be secured by writing to the appropriate embassy in Washington asking for a resident worker visa application. You can scan this text and use it for the license. Of course, the words won't be the right ones for someone who is fluent in the language, but your chance of finding a native speaker of these obscure languages is minuscule.

School ID cards are absolutely the best and most easily manufactured obscure ID available. Literally tens of thousands of schools throughout the United States issue their own ID cards. No one, but no one, is going to know whether the card from Konkolville High School or Sparta Tech is genuine. Too old for a student ID? Issue yourself a faculty card.

Most school ID cards have a picture and Social Security number on them. If the example you have does not include it, use your scanner edit program to make your own. It is illegal to compel people to disclose their Social Security numbers, but a surprising number of schools do so anyway. Pick an obscure place like Noxon, Montana, or Buffalo, Wyoming. Design a card listing full name, address, date of birth, sex, height, weight, and hair and eye color. Include a student ID or Social Security number. In the case of a faculty card, you may wish to devise a code for subjects you teach.

Student IDs are extremely functional when used with a birth certificate to acquire a real Social Security number. They could be used with a homemade birth certificate and Social Security card to acquire a new driver's license, but this might lead to trouble. Fake numbers used on fabricated documents may activate the wrong light in Social Security computers.

Procurement of scannable foreign driver's licenses previously mentioned can be a complex operation requiring a plan all its own. Many foreigners, especially younger students, who come to the United States do not have a national driver's license. Of perhaps 400 national Chinese students the university foreign document collector contacted, *not one* had a Chinese driver's license for him to scan. And a German exchange student said it would cost at least U.S.$2,000 to secure a license to drive legally in Germany; his own plan was to get a much cheaper, easier U.S. driver's license that he intended to trade for a German license on return to Germany. Instead of a birth certificate, he used a standard German identity card to get a U.S. driver's license. These cards (or, more correctly, booklets) are extremely easy to copy with a computer. After learning spoken English and taking the driver's exam, securing a U.S. driver's license using these simple documents is easy and straightforward.

Around Washington, U.S. State Department employees temporarily assigned back to the States trade their Thai, Afghan, Algerian, Chilean, or Malaysian driver's licenses for U.S. ones. Average new IDers attempting this procedure will probably require additional U.S. ID, as well as a pretty good story to go with their request.

The admonition in all these cases is to look beyond the common U.S. driver's license, Social Security cards, business cards, tax forms, library cards, union cards, memberships, credit cards, imprinted check blanks, U.S. birth certificates, baptismal records, and marriage licenses.

There are a lot more official-looking pieces of ID around, which, with the right story, can be parlayed into real ID.

The more obscure the better, in these cases, because those examining the documents won't have a clue about what to look for. The papers you offer may easily be missing vital validating stamps and signatures in their place or origin, but no one here will ever know. You could even come up with a certificate claiming that you are a foreign rocket scientist if that was otherwise wise and profitable.

# 9

# FILING YOUR OWN DEATH CERTIFICATE: THE REAL DEAD END

"It would be so easy," the woman said. "I am shocked to realize that no one ever tried this idea. For seven years I worked in the state bureau of vital statistics, and we never thought about this idea."

"Are you sure no one ever pulled it off and just was never discovered?" I asked.

"Maybe they did," she admitted, "but we never even considered the possibility."

That's from a conversation I had with a local undertaker and his wife. As she said, she had worked for seven years in the state department of health and welfare in the bureau of vital statistics, and he, as an undertaker, was quite familiar with death certificates. The couple found the subject of filing one's own death certificate fascinating.

"There are small variations from state to state, especially relative to getting blank copies of death certificates and of getting back necessary certified copies of deceased nonrelatives. But generally all states use very similar forms," the undertaker said.

Once you have secured a blank copy of a state death certificate, it is relatively easy to fill out and take it to the appropriate local office of a state agency, and then summarily and completely drop off the charts. Undertakers and physicians who fill out death certificates often do so in a rush. Consistency, completeness, or even accuracy do not usually characterize these documents. Some questions, however, are extremely important. Use the wrong buzzwords and officials may become suspicious.

Given proper preparation, staging, timing, and assumption of a reasonably good new ID, it is difficult to impossible for someone to pierce a bogus death certificate—especially if you do not do something foolish, such as claiming a death benefit tying the new you to your old identity. Two steps inhibit investigators trying to do this: (1) they must demonstrate that the death certificate is false, and (2) they must locate the real you. If you "die" in one place and then live in another under a new identity, the chore of locating you is too costly in most cases.

Your first task is to locate a current example of a state death certificate for the state in which you wish to die. About half the 50 states have no restrictions. Simply call at the office of vital statistics and ask for a blank copy of a death certificate. This exercise is valuable in that it will reveal where the completed death certificate is eventually sent or taken when the time comes.

Some states won't issue a blank document but will pass out practically anybody's uncertified copy of his or her filled-in death certificate, which can easily be scanned and reused. Other states are crabby about either blank or completed documents. It is best to call a distant courthouse, ask to be connected to the bureau of vital statistics or public health department, and inquire about both new and used documents. In many cases, it is effective to become the half-brother of the deceased. Distribution to near relatives is easier. What constitutes a near relative is often ill defined.

New, blank certificate forms are easier to work with, but used death certificates can be scanned into a computer system for cleanup and reprinting. Death certificates do not change very often, but it is still wise to get fairly current copies.

At times, current death certificate copies are available from departed family friends or relatives. It doesn't matter who, as long as the form is one in current use, but the state of issue is important. Otherwise we would run a scannable copy in this book. New IDers living, for instance, in the state of Maine won't find much utility in a certificate from Kansas, even though the forms are substantially similar.

Many death certificates are printed in two colors, with red or blue headlines or colored serial numbers. These are basic colors easily picked up by scanners. Undertakers, coroners, and doctors do not place file numbers on documents. Because so many of these forms are handled by so many different hands, serial numbers can be submitted in virtually any order so long as they fall within parameters currently used by the state. Experts point out that many states do not even place serial numbers on their certificates. In most states, numbering is done after completed documents are submitted to state officials. Because we are not interested in receiving certified copies, this numbering is of no consequence.

Other places to find copies of blank death certificates, other than official governmental offices or from deceased family members, include doctors' and coroners' offices and mortuaries. Medical doctors usually don't have blank death certificates in their offices—surprisingly, many doctors have not filled one out in years. On the other hand, some unexpected health professionals have them on hand—for instance, a chiropractor friend of mine keeps them in her office.

At first blush, coroners would seem to be the most difficult people from whom to secure a blank form. In real life this is often not true. Many states do not require a person to have any medical training to be a coroner; if it's an elected position it may pay reasonably well—especially given the few hours of work required.

Because of its nature and perceived status, few people—especially successful medical doctors—will take the job. Often, complete flakes who are party hacks win the position on party line votes. I have secured a blank certificate simply by asking the county coroner in my state's largest city. In most places throughout the United States there are numerous deputy coroners, many of whom can be sweet-talked out of a blank certificate.

Under most circumstances, undertakers are the best source of certificates. In four separate instances spanning three states, I simply walked into a local funeral home and asked for a copy. "I am doing a story on death and dying in the United States," I said. In every case I got a copy, even though state officials responded to written requests by saying that it was impossible to get a blank copy.

The second hurdle before filling in the document involves locating an undertaker's state registration number for use on the certificate. A bogus number can be placed on the appropriate line on the form so long as it generally conforms to style and sequence of those used in the state in which you are attempting to die. However, in most cases, it is wiser to use actual numbers of registered, certified funeral directors. All states maintain a central registry of licensed undertakers in the secretary of state's office. Call these people to find out whether the list also contains their license numbers. Many states also have a state association of funeral directors with offices in the capital city, and inquiries to these people should raise no suspicions.

It is probably safest that you be killed off as an indigent with an address in the worst part of town. Given a year or two, busy funeral homes won't have a clue; their recall of your death will be fuzzy at best. No office record will be available, but this may easily be attributed to sloppy record keeping when the case involves a person of questionable character. Undertakers claim that it really can work this way. Provided that there is no outside evidence that one is still alive, such as an insurance claim, investigators won't really know what to do if the undertaker can't remember.

Most larger states require that attending physicians include their license number on the death certificates they are signing. These numbers are both easier and tougher to locate than you would suppose. A 10-minute search through each of three medical clinics in a given area failed to turn up a state license number. But a 30-second call to a clinic claiming to be a new patient in the city and that "my insurance required a state license number" produced an instant number.

A call to the secretary of state will also produce a list of all medical doctors. In a location with a lot of physicians, it will probably work to make up a name and number of a doctor as long as the number agrees in format and series with those actually in existence. However, making up a name and number from a funeral director is risky, experts warn.

The paper these forms are printed on is *usually* standard, so there is no special challenge here. Some states print legal instructions on the reverse of the form. Either run the form through a Xerox or install the wording from the computer, scanner, and printer.

A recent memo on homemade documents that circulated among bank employees pointed out that a relatively quick and easy method of spotting questionable documents involved looking for missing perforations on edges. Of course, this little slip-up could cause a lot of homemade documents to be spotted, and not just death certificates.

You can manufacture your own perforations at home by carefully running an appropriate document through a sewing machine. Use a small needle set at a fairly thin stitch and, of course, with no thread. You must keep the line perfectly straight. Clamping the document to a thin piece of cardboard and then taping a guide to the machine table is often helpful for this.

A death certificate will likely contain the following information, although not necessarily in the order presented here. Some items may not appear at all on some states' forms. Basically, use the following operational philosophy to gain credibility. Most death certificates are filled out in longhand.

1. *Decedent's name.* Place the full name and middle initial of the person who is being killed off.

2. *Social Security number.* Often this is not filled out because too few people used to have them, and today this information is not immediately available to the undertaker or physician. Many people under a deadline to get the certificate filled out are too busy or too lazy to check for Social Security numbers. In any event, it is common to leave this line blank; or if it is helpful, place your old number on the line. Several states do not check these numbers. Inserting any number would work as long as it looks valid and there is nothing suspicious about it that leads to verification.

3. *Date of death.* Put down whatever works. Lines are usually provided for infants, which do not apply in your case. Funeral directors claim it is best to wait three or

four months after disappearing before filing a personal death certificate, and to do so in a medium-to-large city far from from where you have taken up your new residence. Undertakers do not have to live near the deceased as long as they are in the same state.

4. *Date and place of birth.* Use your own information or make it up, but don't forget that investigators may confirm that it is indeed you by date of birth and Social Security number. If possible, list a foreign country as a place of birth. Investigators are really stymied by this ploy.

5. *Military service.* Yes or no. Most states now ask because Uncle Sam provides some burial benefits if the decedent qualifies for them and a member of the family or authorized agency applies for them. It is best to stay away from this additional inquiry. No is your choice.

6. *Place of death.* This is a critical question because investigators will attempt to track the deceased down through the address given. If a private residence is listed and it appears death may have occurred unattended, the state may look for a coroner's signature. A sheriff may even be sent out to investigate. Note that this is place of death and not last residence.

You sometimes have to list the place of death, but in some cases you may simply check an appropriate box, such as inpatient/outpatient facility, emergency room, DOA (usually resulting from an accident or crime), long-term care facility, own residence, other private residence, or other applicable answer.

Experts say that listing long-term care facility is by far the best way to go because fewer questions are asked and a coroner's signature is not required. Theoretically, any doctor can attend to any patient in any long-term care facility. Registering clerks may not recognize the doctor's name on the document, but this is of no concern.

Pick a low-end retirement center or long-term health care facility from the phone book and list it. In most cases, it is wise to walk or drive by to determine whether the facility is run down, which gives the impression that lots of folks are moving through the place on a steady basis.

7. *Marital information.* In this space, list the ex-spouse you may be attempting to ditch, leave it blank, or make up a name—whichever seems to generate the least inquiry. If an ex might travel to the far city where you "die" and unravel your scheme, list a false name, putting *deceased* in parentheses behind the name. Questions regarding maiden name and parents can simply be left blank. No one checks these lines out.

8. *Racial and ethnic information.* There will be some questions on race and family origin. Given the status of current federal regulations, funeral directors claim it is not necessary to fill out these blanks. (Large portions of many death certificates are routinely left blank.)

9. *Occupation.* This should always be something as innocuous as electrician, farmer, factory worker, pressman, or truck driver. Do *not* put private investigator, soldier of fortune, police officer, educator, politician,

or other high-profile occupation of the type that might generate publicity.

10. *Parents.* Whenever a separate line appears, leave it blank or put in whatever you please. This is what most funeral directors do. State officials have little or no means of checking this information.

11. *Informant.* This refers to the person who found the body or called the funeral home at the time of death. Pick the manager of a care center if you can out find a name, somebody at random from the phone book, somebody from the obituary column of the paper, or somebody whose name will likely soon appear in the obituary column. Make this as much of a dead end as possible, while still retaining credibility (don't list Hillary Clinton, for example).

12. *Former residence of deceased.* This is very important. Pick a cheap, shabby flophouse-type rental in the wrong part of town, notorious for the large number of people who come and go. List the name of the complex, address, and county, as requested. Keep in mind that this address should not be anywhere near your current location as a new ID.

13. *Disposition and name and address of funeral director.* This should be an existing funeral director with a real address. Pick one from a directory whose license number is available. It need not be a local firm, as long as the address is within the state chosen for death.

14. *Disposition of the body.* This too is an extremely important set of information. Cremation must be listed so that no one starts looking for a body and so that no listing for a cemetery is necessary. Many

states require a transportation and cemetery permit if interment is indicated.

15. *Cause of death.* As with some previous questions, this one must be filled in appropriately to avoid undue investigation. If this blank is improperly done, immediate suspicion will result. Medical statisticians frequently look at this information. In no case should death be attributed to an accident. Unattended deaths must be countersigned by the coroner in most states.

   It is best to list trendy, fast-acting conditions such as hepatic failure due to alcohol abuse, or lung cancer from tobacco abuse. Make sure that if it is you being killed off that cause of death matches your previous life-style and personality. One fellow said that he wanted to die at the hand of a jealous husband, but in this case that listing would be folly.

16. *Time and day of month of death.* Be sure to make this entry plausible.

17. *Certifier information.* This is the line that either a doctor or coroner must sign. Since there are far more medical doctors than coroners out there, be a medical doctor. This is also an excuse for notoriously bad handwriting. Practice reproducing a very rough, obscure signature of a medical doctor in the area. It need not look much like the original! With a bit of practice, even a handprinted signature can be made to look uncertain.

   If, by some stroke of fortune, a fairly recent obituary can be found in the local paper for a doctor, use his or her name on the certificate. Signed and dated even a week before the doctor's death, this will provide a virtually insurmountable obstacle to investigators, all other things being equal.

Numerous other lines may be provided for information relative to death by accident. Leave these blank. It is not wise to bring in additional phony signatures of investigating officers and, as mentioned, coroners.

18. *Registrar's signature.* This is the last and sometimes the most difficult signature. Registrars are located in the bureau of vital statistics in the county courthouse. Many larger communities have several satellite offices, and in some states there are regional offices. In medium-to-large communities, a number of different people can sign as registrar, greatly simplifying the process. Office locations of local registrars are easily obtained by calling either the department of health and welfare or the secretary of state.

Completed documents are carried personally or, in the case of larger communities, mailed to the registrar. (In smaller communities, the registrar or office receptionist may know everyone, so it is best that death occurs in a medium-to-large community.) Since registrars sign the document and stamp it, agents of the funeral director take the document in for signature and stamping and then return with certified copies.

Many funeral directors just send the document to the correct office; doing this will require that an envelope with a plausible return address be manufactured. Experts claim that this can simply be a high-quality, plain envelope with a typed return address or a very fancy, computer-generated, printed envelope. Since you do not want certified copies, sending is as good as taking it in.

At any rate, take or send the homemade death certificate to the registrar. It will be signed and filed. Some offices hold these certificates locally for up to two years. For this time you are legally dead, at least on paper.

Fortunately, all of the bureaucratic lines on the graph never seem to line up. In states where it is tough to get a recent copy of a death certificate, undertakers or doctors seem to have blank copies freely available. Where death certificates for everyone are available for the asking, coming by a blank seems to be tough. So far, I have been able to scrounge up something in almost all states, in most cases simply by writing or calling their bureaus of vital statistics at the state capitals or by asking undertakers. In both Texas and Indiana, I was told that securing a blank certificate was completely impossible, but undertakers quickly provided copies.

*Do not, under any circumstances, attempt to file a homemade death certificate on yourself if insurance money is involved.* Even if it is a relatively modest amount, problems will certainly result. Insurance companies, unlike bureaucrats, will actually attempt to investigate any claim that seems questionable. Bureaucrats can spend money on investigations without end, but the quality of their people is never as good as in the private sector and they are not similarly motivated.

Customarily, the undertaker asks for several certified copies of the document for use with the IRS, banks, insurance companies, or whatever. For our purposes, these certified copies are unnecessary. In fact, one weakness of this way of doing things involves *not* asking for certified copies. When you kill yourself on paper, you are going as a friendless, penniless pauper who drank his liver to death in a cheap flophouse. No one even knows where your ashes reside. No certified copies are needed in cases like yours.

Some few funeral directors file statements of death with the Social Security Administration. This is the form that retires the deceased's Social Security number. In some sections of the country, funeral directors almost never file this form, while in others it is virtually universal. Many surviving relatives do not even know that a filing can be requested.

Unless for some reason you wish also to cancel your Social Security number, as added evidence of your demise, filing is unnecessary or perhaps even inadvisable.

Most death certificates have a second or even third sheet having to do with authorization to transport the body or notifying the cemetery. There is no need to fool with these. You are simply legally killing yourself off, not authorizing transport of your body. All that is required is filling out and filing the one form with the local office of the state bureau of vital statistics.

Dying by using the previous device has a great deal of charm. It is quick and easy. Given that you are off someplace else, living under a complete new ID, it provides a solid investigative dead end. These death certificates lead to a completely invalid location with no further leads to follow even if the investigator does smell a rat.

As a kind of coup de grace, make up a brief obituary on yourself for insertion in the local paper in the city in which you once lived. Look in current papers for obituaries, which could be copied almost verbatim, with your substituting only basic personal data.

As a service to the bereaved, funeral homes usually send short obituaries to the deceased's hometown paper. About half the papers run these free of charge as a service, if they are brief; others charge a nominal amount. Call the appropriate newspaper for price and policy information. Obituaries and death notices can be typed on plain paper without raising suspicions, or they can be produced on nice funeral home letterhead on a computer. Place cash in the envelope if payment is required.

On a random basis, hometown papers will call the funeral home in a distant city to confirm the death of a native son for whom they have received an obituary.

Undertakers know of no valid method of predicting when these confirming calls will be made.

If telephone numbers are included on the letterhead, the paper will call that number rather than checking with information. If the call is placed from a great distance (two or three states away), the secretary at the paper will have no idea what city the signal is reaching. Yet it could be very compromising to list a number that could someday to traced to an individual. Rather than throwing the letter away after publication, the paper may keep it and the phone number on file.

Consider deploying a street or convenience store pay phone as your office number of the Cedar Hills funeral home. Obituaries are run very quickly. Waiting for two days after the letter hits the paper is probably adequate. Wise men will pick a spot where this sort of waiting is inconspicuous: remember, some communities believe they are waging war on drugs by limiting opportunities to answer pay phones.

A friendly undertaker, who provided much of the previous information regarding death certificates, says he would go one step further if he decided to become a new ID. This fellow, who is comfortable around computers, said, "I would use my desktop publishing system to create a totally new marriage license using my new fictitious name, married to a totally fictitious woman. Then I would file a death certificate on her, leaving me as the remaining widowed husband."

**INDIANA STATE DEPARTMENT OF HEALTH**
**VITAL RECORDS SECTION**
1330 West Michigan Street
P.O. Box 1964
Indianapolis, IN 46206-1964

MR# _____ Date Rec'd _____

☐ Your fee of $_____ was received and is being held pending return of information requested below.

☐ Please remit additional fee of $_____

---

### DEATH RECORDS IN THE STATE VITAL RECORDS OFFICE BEGIN WITH 1900

Death Registration in Indiana began in 1882. Prior to 1900, records of death are filed ONLY with the Local Health Department in the county where the death actually occurred.

There are no indexes to the state death certificates from 1900 through 1918. The specific CITY or COUNTY of death must be provided for searches in this period and the search is limited to one county for each Search Fee ($4.00) paid.

---

**Application for Search and Certified Copy of Death Record**
**Please Complete All Items Below**

Was this a
stillbirth? _____

Name of Deceased _____

Date of Death _____

Place of Death (City) _____ (County) _____ INDIANA

**SEARCH FEE - $4.00:** If the exact date of death is not known, please indicate the five (5) year period to be searched. An additional $4.00 is required for **each additional five (5) year period searched, or COUNTY SEARCHED from 1900-1918.** Search fees are nonrefundable.

Date of birth of deceased (if known) _____

Father's Name _____ Mother's Maiden Name _____

Your relationship to the person named on this record? _____

Purpose for which the record is to be used? _____

**Signature of Applicant** _____

Printed Name of Applicant _____

Street Address _____

City _____ State _____ Zip Code _____

Telephone Number _____

Total Certificates: _____ Total Fee: $_____

State Form 36174
SDH06-023
Rev. 9/92  VRFORM11/VR1

---

Indiana State Department of Health Vital Records Section application for a search and certified copy of death certificate.

## STATEMENT OF DEATH BY FUNERAL DIRECTOR

| NAME OF DECEASED | SOCIAL SECURITY NUMBER |
|---|---|

Please complete the items below, and return the form in the enclosed addressed, postage paid envelope. Your assistance and cooperation are appreciated.

PAPERWORK ACT NOTICE: The information on this form is authorized by sections 404.715 and 404.720 of Federal Regulations (20 CFR 404.715 and 404.720). While your response is voluntary, we need your assistance to make an accurate and timely determination concerning the death of the individual named above, and to determine if there are survivors who may be eligible for Social Security benefits.

We may also use the information you give us when we match records by computer. Matching programs compare our records with those of other Federal, State, or local government agencies. Many agencies may use matching programs to find or prove that a person qualifies for benefits paid by the Federal government. The law allows us to do this even if you do not agree to it.

Explanations about these and other reasons why information you provide us may be used or given out are available in Social Security offices. If you want to learn more about this, contact any Social Security office.

TIME IT TAKES TO COMPLETE THIS FORM

We estimate that it will take you about 3.5 minutes to complete this form. This includes the time it will take to read the instructions, gather the necessary facts and fill out the form. If you have comments or suggestions on this estimate, or on any other aspect of this form, write to the Social Security Administration, ATTN: Reports Clearance Officer, 1-A-21 Operations Bldg., Baltimore, MD 21235-0001, and to the Office of Management and Budget, Paperwork Reduction Project (0960-0138), Washington, D.C. 20503. Send only comments relating to our estimate or other aspects of this form to the offices listed above. All requests for Social Security cards and other claims-related information should be sent to your local Social Security office, whose address is listed in your telephone directory under the Department of Health and Human Services.

| 1. NAME OF DECEASED | | 2. SOCIAL SECURITY NUMBER __ __ __ / __ __ / __ __ __ __ |
|---|---|---|
| 3. DATE OF DEATH | 4. DATE OF BIRTH (if known) | 5. Check (✓) whether the deceased was ☐ Male ☐ Female |

6. NAME OF WIDOW OR WIDOWER (if known)

7. ADDRESS (No. and Street, P.O. Box) OF WIDOW OR WIDOWER (if known)

| CITY | STATE | ZIP CODE | TELEPHONE NUMBER (if Available) (area code) |
|---|---|---|---|

I hereby certify that I am an authorized funeral director and prepared for final disposition the body of the person named above. I understand this statement may be used in connection with an application for Social Security benefits.

| NAME AND ADDRESS OF FUNERAL DIRECTOR OR FIRM | SIGNATURE OF FUNERAL DIRECTOR OR AUTHORIZED REPRESENTATIVE |
|---|---|
| | TELEPHONE NUMBER (area code) / DATE |

FOR SOCIAL SECURITY USE ONLY – DO NOT WRITE IN THIS SPACE

Form SSA-721 (9-91) Destroy prior editions

Department of Health and Human Services Social Security Administration Statement of Death by Funeral Director form.

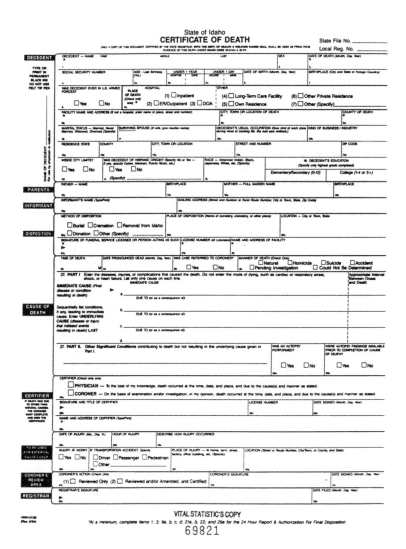

State of Idaho Certificate of Death form.

**CERTIFICATE OF DEATH**
STATE OF CALIFORNIA
USE BLACK INK ONLY/NO ERASURES, WHITEOUTS OR ALTERATIONS
VS-11 (REV. 7/93)

STATE FILE NUMBER

LOCAL REGISTRATION NUMBER

| | | |
|---|---|---|
| 1. NAME OF DECEDENT—FIRST (GIVEN) | 2. MIDDLE | 3. LAST (FAMILY) |

**DECEDENT PERSONAL DATA**

| 4. DATE OF BIRTH MM/DD/CCYY | 5. AGE YRS. | IF UNDER 1 YEAR — MONTHS | DAYS | IF UNDER 24 HOURS — HOURS | MINUTES | 6. SEX | 7. DATE OF DEATH MM/DD/CCYY | 8. HOUR |
|---|---|---|---|---|---|---|---|---|

| 9. STATE OF BIRTH | 10. SOCIAL SECURITY NO. | 11. MILITARY SERVICE 19 ___ TO 19 ___ NONE | 12. MARITAL STATUS | 13. EDUCATION —YEARS COMPLETED |
|---|---|---|---|---|

| 14. RACE | 15. HISPANIC—SPECIFY YES NO | 16. USUAL EMPLOYER |
|---|---|---|

| 17. OCCUPATION | 18. KIND OF BUSINESS | 19. YEARS IN OCCUPATION |
|---|---|---|

**USUAL RESIDENCE**

20. RESIDENCE—STREET AND NUMBER OR LOCATION

| 21. CITY | 22. COUNTY | 23. ZIP CODE | 24. YRS IN COUNTY | 25. STATE OR FOREIGN COUNTRY |
|---|---|---|---|---|

**INFORMANT**

| 26. NAME, RELATIONSHIP | 27. MAILING ADDRESS (STREET AND NUMBER OR RURAL ROUTE NUMBER, CITY OR TOWN, STATE, ZIP) |
|---|---|

**SPOUSE AND PARENT INFORMATION**

| 28. NAME OF SURVIVING SPOUSE—FIRST | 29. MIDDLE | 30. LAST (MAIDEN NAME) | |
|---|---|---|---|
| 31. NAME OF FATHER—FIRST | 32. MIDDLE | 33. LAST | 34. BIRTH STATE |
| 35. NAME OF MOTHER—FIRST | 36. MIDDLE | 37. LAST (MAIDEN) | 38. BIRTH STATE |

**DISPOSITION(S)**

| 39. DATE MM/DD/CCYY | 40. PLACE OF FINAL DISPOSITION |
|---|---|

**FUNERAL DIRECTOR AND LOCAL REGISTRAR**

| 41. TYPE OF DISPOSITION(S) | 42. SIGNATURE OF EMBALMER | 43. LICENSE NO. |
|---|---|---|
| 44. NAME OF FUNERAL DIRECTOR | 45. LICENSE NO. 46. SIGNATURE OF OCA REGISTRAR | 47. DATE MM/DD/CCYY |

**PLACE OF DEATH**

| 101. PLACE OF DEATH | 102. IF HOSP, SPECIFY ONE: IP EM/OP DOA | 103. FACILITY OTHER THAN HOSPITAL: CONV. HOSP. RES. OTHER | 104. COUNTY |
|---|---|---|---|
| 105. STREET ADDRESS—STREET AND NUMBER OR LOCATION | | | 106. CITY |

**CAUSE OF DEATH**

| 107. DEATH WAS CAUSED BY: (ENTER ONLY ONE CAUSE PER LINE FOR A, B, C, AND D) | TIME INTERVAL BETWEEN ONSET AND DEATH | 108. DEATH REPORTED TO CORONER YES NO REFERRAL NUMBER |
|---|---|---|
| IMMEDIATE CAUSE (A) | | 109. BIOPSY PERFORMED YES NO |
| DUE TO (B) | | 110. AUTOPSY PERFORMED YES NO |
| DUE TO (C) | | 111. USED IN DETERMINING CAUSE YES NO |
| DUE TO (D) | | |

112. OTHER SIGNIFICANT CONDITIONS CONTRIBUTING TO DEATH BUT NOT RELATED TO CAUSE GIVEN IN 107

113. WAS OPERATION PERFORMED FOR ANY CONDITION IN ITEM 107 OR 112? IF YES, LIST TYPE OF OPERATION AND DATE.

**PHYSICIAN'S CERTIFICATION**

| 114. I CERTIFY THAT TO THE BEST OF MY KNOWLEDGE DEATH OCCURRED AT THE HOUR, DATE AND PLACE STATED FROM THE CAUSES STATED. DECEDENT ATTENDED SINCE MM/DD/CCYY DECEDENT LAST SEEN ALIVE MM/DD/CCYY | 115. SIGNATURE AND TITLE OF CERTIFIER | 116. LICENSE NO. | 117. DATE MM/DD/CCYY |
|---|---|---|---|
| | 118. TYPE ATTENDING PHYSICIAN'S NAME, MAILING ADDRESS · ZIP | | |

**CORONER'S USE ONLY**

| I CERTIFY THAT IN MY OPINION DEATH OCCURRED AT THE HOUR, DATE AND PLACE STATED FROM THE CAUSES STATED. 119. MANNER OF DEATH NATURAL SUICIDE HOMICIDE ACCIDENT PENDING INVESTIGATION COULD NOT BE DETERMINED | 120. INJURY AT WORK YES NO | 121. INJURY DATE MM/DD/CCYY | 122. HOUR | 123. PLACE OF INJURY |
|---|---|---|---|---|
| | 124. DESCRIBE HOW INJURY OCCURRED (EVENTS WHICH RESULTED IN INJURY) | | | |

125. LOCATION (STREET AND NUMBER OR LOCATION AND CITY AND ZIP CODE)

| 126. SIGNATURE OF CORONER OR DEPUTY CORONER | 127. DATE MM/DD/CCYY | 128. TYPED NAME, TITLE OF CORONER OR DEPUTY CORONER |
|---|---|---|

**STATE REGISTRAR**

| A | B | C | D | E | F | G | H | FAX AUTH. # | CENSUS TRACT |
|---|---|---|---|---|---|---|---|---|---|

State of California Certificate of Death form.

# 10

# THE BLACK ECONOMY

In 1986 Mark McCormack, a wildly successful businessman, wrote a book entitled *What They Don't Teach You at Harvard Business School*. Full of pithy, simple little observations that successful people usually take for granted but seldom verbalize, this volume became a best-seller.

This chapter of my book is the part that they don't tell you about in conventional books about new identity. Conventional writers just seem to take for granted the fact that everybody has to work for a living. In the same breath they point out that successful new IDers can't possibly work for an employer who demands identification, nor can they safely accept public assistance.

The dilemma is that a person must remain quietly, gainfully employed to remain hidden. But employment is one of the best and easiest pipelines available to pursuing investigators. Good old, new IDer Floyd set me on to this philosophy, which he pointed out is never, ever even mentioned in other new ID books. "My ex-wife thought she could find me immediately," he said, "because I won't live like a snake, and my work skills are kind of unique."

Additionally, my experience as an investigator confirms that a person cannot go on welfare and remain securely hidden. Under our predominantly conservative legislators, welfare recipients are being increasingly scrutinized. Isn't one of the best methods of cutting welfare costs to cut cheating?

Public assistance workers are not supposed to talk about their wards, but good investigators always manage to secure this information. Social Security number-based data banks make it very easy to track people on public assistance. "But, I will hide behind a new name and Social Security number," you say. This may work for a time, or it may simply add another layer of folks trying to uncover you.

Working to secure an adequate income while hiding is essential. It has not, until recently, been easy to do so and still keep off employers' books. As mentioned, determined new IDers cannot work in their former occupations or anyplace "official" where they receive a regular company paycheck—not until they have success-fully fashioned a completely new identity including a Social Security number.

Part of your departure plan must include carrying along enough cash to live—ideally, for up to one year. As detailed earlier, living expenses for a year, including the purchase of needed computers and a vehicle, will run upwards of $20,000. Even with this stash, the time will quickly arrive when cash-producing labor is essential. What to do? Is this an insoluble dilemma for aspiring new IDers?

Many, if not most, American economists now recognize that after combined taxes eat up in excess of 35 percent of a person's income, the incentive to work off the books becomes almost irresistible. As proof, they tell us to look at the impact of raising the tax rate to 40 percent. Relatively little additional money is raised, and certainly not 5 percent more than was collected at the 35 percent rate.

Universally, people take protective measures to insulate themselves from these increased taxes—a truth politicians seem unable or unwilling to grasp. People decide to work less, hire attorneys and accountants to find loopholes, find more deductions, change their income pattern, or, as is often true with working-class folks who see no choice, work in the underground economy. Raise tax rates high enough and people completely drop out of the tax-paying economy. This explains why economic vibrancy in places such as Canada, Italy, Brazil, and Thailand are dramatically understated by official figures.

In many Third World countries where taxes are usurious, the black economy is the only thing keeping the country going. Sometimes, politicians tacitly recognize this truth by allowing the black economy to continue. To a limited extent, this is currently the situation in the inner city in the United States. U.S. taxmen work harder to uncover welfare fraud and drug sales than they do to thwart cash economy entrepreneurs.

Current U.S. tax policy is wonderful for new IDers. Total taxes—federal, state, and local—stand at around 47 percent! Like any good Third World economy, people are flocking by the scores into the more profitable underground economy. You won't raise any suspicions among common citizens if that is how you decide to live.

"Pay cash," four students recently said, "and we will paint your house for 30 percent less money." And, as mentioned earlier, an acquaintance's housekeeper informed him that she was getting a divorce and needed more money but proposed that if he paid in cash she'd continue at the same rate.

Omer Betten was an old, wizened, hunched-over man who walked with a pronounced limp. I don't know if he was a new IDer or what it was. Omer (not *Homer*, if you please) lived in a tiny, one-room shack about a mile from our farm. Dead and dying lawn mowers at least 11 deep surrounded his shack. With their handles sticking up obscenely, they personified material ugliness. No one knew very much about Omer—such as where he had come from, who his folks were, or even how he made his living.

Because my old, klutzy chainsaw often needed repairs, I got to know Omer as well as anybody thereabouts. One day while we were working together, he mentioned that anyone who could repair tools with small engines could make a living anywhere. "I've traveled an awful lot in my day," he said. "Wherever I settle down, I can earn a living. Everyone needs to be able to do that," he said. "At one time I cut hair and another I cobbled shoes, but engine repair is the best," he said. "I can always make good money doing that."

I was tempted to point out that obviously it isn't what you make, but what you spend, that counts. Instead, I silently agreed. It was the only time he ever alluded to his past.

New IDer Floyd went to work immediately as soon as he settled in at his new residence, and always for cash. At first he couldn't find anything else, so he did industrial cleaning for a fellow who had several contracts in the city in which Floyd landed. The contractor was interested in cheap, reliable help, not in Social Security numbers and name verification. Without friends, family, and other job-related responsibilities, Floyd had a great deal of extra time to dink around with his computer system. Among other things, he designed and printed a number of cards and letterheads for various businesses that ranged from shoveling sidewalks to preparing people's taxes.

Floyd's example is not to say that running a cleaning service is not honorable or profitable. A friend's daughter, for instance, hauled in $10,800 tax free in 14 months cleaning houses. Demand for this service is excellent, as is the money. But Floyd thought he could profitably undertake several other ventures, so he wanted numerous different identifications, and he wanted to shake out his computer.

After trying his hand at cleaning, he prepared tax returns. But tax season ended, and Floyd thought an eight-week stay south of the border would do wonders for the morale of those chasing him. He worked on a real estate deal involving several wealthy Mexicans. Floyd would not have dared do real estate deals in the United States, because this had been his occupation in his former life. He reckoned the occupation was safe enough in Mexico.

New IDer Ken has two methods of generating income. Principally, he peddles copies of his book at gun shows and conferences. As a backup, he restores old motorcycles and does intricate mechanical work on old Harleys for cash.

It is always easy to find cash employment in the service industry. The April 4, 1995, *Wall Street Journal* carried an article entitled "Off the books—For inner Detroit the hidden economy is crucial part of life." This article graphically pointed out that people who can do plumbing repairs, fix leaky roofs, or restore termite-ridden porches will always find work. One man who worked on a Ford Motor Company assembly line for many years reports that he finds greater satisfaction and income doing odd jobs for people in his neighborhood. Not only is he no longer bored out of his tree, the money is reasonably good.

Most of the jobs these cash workers handle seem little more complex than tasks performed by regular homeowners in the course of keeping their house in repair. Our featured handyman admits that he often does not know when he gets up in the morning what jobs will come in. But the fellow reportedly is quite happy and has enough income to provide a comfortable existence.

Although work in the service sector of the underground economy may be easy to find, it may not always be wise. Dentists from Tucson, for instance, who move to Fort Wayne to engage in the same occupation will probably be discovered. Again this depends to an extent on how badly somebody wants your behind. If really deep cover is indicated, and you were in construction at any time in your past, you should probably not even work as a contractor's estimator on drywall jobs or in a building supply outlet. This is not to suggest that a new IDer drywaller could not work as a plumber, tile installer, or any of the many other construction-related occupations— only that, like Floyd, intelligent consideration must be given before jumping in. Having a few bucks in reserve will help ensure that decisions are made rationally rather than out of necessity.

Certain traditionally transitional occupations such as waiter, short-order cook, or car washer are not nearly as unregulated as they once were. Some new IDers have applied for these jobs and, when asked for Social Security numbers, have been forced to give fake ones. Under these conditions, they seldom actually show up for work. When they do, they stay only a month or two.

Some people believe that it is safe to work three or four months for a company, using a false name and Social Security number. When the boss or other employees start to question your story or your past, then it is time to move down the street to the next job, they insist. Actual working new IDers are leery of this measure because it may needlessly set in motion the wheels of inquiry.

Miller is not really a hard-core new IDer, but he did intentionally leave the place of his birth to start a radically new, different life. By incredible luck or wise design, he picked a state having strict licensing laws about construction work. Supposedly, he has to be tested and evaluated by a board of contractors before he can work in construction.

Miller believes that these laws are actually intended to grant monopoly powers to those with licenses and to keep people out of the cash economy. As a result, homeowners find that little construction jobs requiring minimal skill and maximum ambition, such as hanging doors or replacing gutters, are usuriously expensive.

Unless he desperately needs work, Miller only takes smaller jobs. If necessary, he breaks larger jobs into $999 increments to satisfy local authorities and to avoid their scrutiny. So far he has had plenty of lucrative contracts. In that regard, he suggests picking a tightly regulated occupation in an autocratic state and city. As an aside, he pays *all* his bills in cash. At times, he says, it is inconvenient not being able to run money through a checking account, but he has acclimated to carrying around a roll of money. In this day and age, vendors are not even surprised, he observes. Rather than leaving a paper trail by charging materials, he pays cash and receives a nice additional discount in the process.

Fortunately for new IDers who must work to remain hidden, our society is increasingly tolerant of this cash economy.

Floyd, the new IDer who cleaned offices, prepared taxes, and then went to Mexico, eventually found that his skills as an office manager kept him employed, even without documentation. He felt that this job classification was broad enough that he was not risking discovery after a year of deep cover. He hired on as an independent consultant, with few questions asked, providing yet another example of hard-pressed employers willing to save money by hiring undocumented workers as long as they bring valuable skills. The IRS is trying to change the system, but, currently, consultants in this country have great independence.

New IDer Ken strongly recommends mechanic work for those struggling to rustle up a few dollars in the cash economy. Most garages now figure from $75 to $100 per hour gross on labor. This includes shop rate and parts markup. Brake and muffler jobs are the most common repairs, both of which require only a modest level of skill, he concludes.

Bill isn't really a new IDer but, because of past business dealings, he is continually on the run from creditors. To escape judgments, he finds he must deal exclusively in the cash economy. His current income comes entirely from proofreading people's manuscripts and setting up computer-driven desktop publishing systems.

"Home computer systems are now virtually ubiquitous," he says. "But most first-time owners chicken out too quickly. I step in and, for $100 cash, hook everything up, get it all running together, and then teach the neophyte basic computer use."

Bill is probably exaggerating when he claims that every third American has a book they want published. He does, however, make quite a bit of cash editing and laying out copy for aspiring authors.

The list of potential occupations and job skills available in the cash economy is endless. The *Wall Street Journal* article on the underground economy reports that some people even make fees on such mundane work as cashing checks for old or shut-in people who live in high-crime areas. Other employment suggestions include—but are not limited to—work as a welder, bridge painter, bulldozer operator, photographer, driver, data entry person, clown, farmhand, gardener, truck driver, and trash hauler. All new IDers interviewed suggested that new IDers practice working in the cash economy for at least six months *before* they disappear.

Will isn't a new IDer, but he does work in the underground economy. Just over four years ago, he started handing out cards for a service named Me and My Truck. For modest cash fees, he offered to bring his battered, old, red 1978 Chevy quarter-ton around to haul away virtually anything you want hauled. Now Will drives a brand-new truck (he doesn't say which kind or color) and farms out overflow jobs to two friends. When asked how he managed to write his truck off on his income taxes, he just smiles broadly.

New IDer Ken knows of a fellow in deep trouble at home who quickly and quietly joined a combine crew harvesting across the nation. He worked 12 hours per day, seven days a week for three months in places where authorities seldom look. He couldn't be found because he told no one about his plan. All his eating and sleeping expenses were covered, and at the end he had saved enough money to live without working for at least three or four months. He stayed in the little burg in North Dakota when the harvest company disbanded there. By that time, authorities had pretty well burned themselves out looking for him. They gave up on him, at least in an active sense. His was an especially good plan because this fellow moved from place to place in rural areas, far from anyone—much less the authorities. His boss did ask for a Social Security number, but the fellow felt safe listing one that was false. His boss only filed once every two to three months. By the time his boss filed, he—the new IDer—was long gone. Ken does not know to what extent this fellow manufactured new documents at his new residence in North Dakota.

While he was working for the company, several of the fellow's co-workers were arrested for public drunkenness. Had he been among them his cover would have been blown, big time. Universally, new IDers stress that it is complete insanity to engage in criminal activities of any kind, beyond remaining gainfully employed in the cash economy. Each cites case after case of people who ran scam operations, dealt drugs, or even robbed 7-11 stores, and were instantly exposed and caught. Given modern computers, crime patterns will lead back to their former selves. It's an instant invitation for investigators to start asking unwanted questions.

You were a lazy, ignorant bum in your old life? Forget about remaining out of the authorities' clutches for very long in a new ID. Intelligent, diligent, hard-working people can, however, pull it off nicely—in spite of the fact that some heavy-duty people are out there looking for them.

# 11

# AN
# ON-THE-GROUND
# PLAN OF ACTION

Recently, the local police radio squawked to life with the jolly fact that two young women were in the process of being overtaken and stopped by a sheriff's department deputy because of "erratic driving." Of course, this could have been a setup on the part of the gendarmes, but it seemed from the radio traffic that something may have been genuinely amiss.

Reportedly, the "car with contents" (the two women) was weaving from center stripe to side stripe, barely keeping alignment down the right of way. On first seeing the cop, the driver zoomed ahead over a little hill, where she immediately pulled into a narrow farm field access path. She had barely stopped when she threw open the door and attempted to run around to the passenger side to change positions with her companion. The undersheriff reported this amateur running and hiding in a most incredulous tone on the radio.

On checking their driver's licenses, the sheriff observed that the real driver was under indictment in another state on a drug charge, was probably jumping bail, and was definitely driving on a suspended license. Although no one is admitting anything, the two ladies could well have been on their way out of town in search of a new ID.

Getting picked up for erratic driving at 11:00 in the morning is definitely not a good way to start a new ID program if, in fact, that is what they were doing. For starters, experienced, successful new IDers claim that acquiring a new ID is seldom, if ever, a togetherness project. Apparently, there are absolutely no examples on record of even a husband and wife dropping off government wanted lists together. Only if the couple completely leaves the country, expert people finders claim, can two people ever drop out. This is the case because their unique footprints of personal characteristics will always lead back to their former selves. Two people together can always easily be found unless they quietly move to Canada or Mexico, or take a private vessel to Tahiti.

But back to the issue at hand: planning the great escape and acquiring a new ID. Assuming that you have finally had it with our justice system or socioeconomic conditions, what precisely should you do? The following plan incorporates all the lessons taught in the previous chapters into a comprehensive, stretch-to-fit escape plan. However, remember that all situations are somewhat different and that certain variables will determine what will and will not fit in specific situations. Among the most critical variables are the following:

1. The reasons for your flight
2. The intensity of the pursuit
3. The amount of time you have had to prepare for your departure and your commitment to planning for it
4. Your ability to keep your intentions and any possible destinations a secret from *everybody*
5. The amount of money you have to take with you and your ability to assume a new career in the black economy
6. Your access to equipment to home-manufacture new ID documents
7. Your level of expertise at extorting legal ID papers from the system
8. Your willingness to cut *all* ties with your previous life and make yourself over into a totally new person

After assessing your situation, it is up to you to come up with a plan for your new identity. The following is intended as a guide only.

## ASSEMBLE YOUR COMPUTER SYSTEM AND SCAN IN SAMPLE DOCUMENTS

Before leaving, spend time assembling the computer system described in Chapter 4 to duplicate documents, including a computer, scanner, color printer, correct interface cords, editing program, and operating system. New IDers may not be able to take all this equipment with them, but the experience of actually pulling all of this together and getting it to work is invaluable.

Scan into the computer as many official documents as you can lay your hands on. Do everything from your aunt's death certificate to your sister's student ID to birth certificates for your spouse, father, mother, and siblings. Be voracious and thorough about collecting and scanning every ID document within your reach, including library cards, INS documents, driver's licenses, and Social Security cards. Keep careful records about weight, color, and grade of paper used to replicate each document. Store on duplicate disks (or a removable hard drive), allowing you a permanent backup. Computer disks are, of course, very compact, allowing you to pack along a huge amount of information. Avoid placing any of your new ID material on your internal hard-disk drive unless you will be taking your computer (or this drive) with you. Merely erasing files from your hard disk won't remove them completely, and reformatting your hard disk before you leave town—though it would erase the record of your new-ID materials—might also raise a lot of pesky questions.

### ARRANGE YOUR TRANSPORTATION, DESTINATION, AND ENTRY DOCUMENTS

Manufacture an international driver's license and a few supporting ID items such as business cards and an overseas youth (or senior) hostel card with which to get out of town. Keep in mind that these documents will probably not pass muster if you get stopped by a cop or attempt to use them with someone who is suspicious of you. You should probably use an interim persona when actually making your move.

Withdraw all your cash reserves from their holding places. If there isn't enough money, your move will probably be unsuccessful.

At a neighboring city, purchase an alternative vehicle for cash from a used-car dealer. As a general working rule, taking public transport out of town won't work for several reasons. Your departure will be timed and duly noted by ticket sellers and takers. Carrying along necessary items needed for a new life is also virtually impossible, especially when keeping a low profile.

While the dealer completes necessary paperwork and prepares your "new" vehicle, drive down to the motor vehicle department to secure a new set of legal license plates and a new title. Titles are usually returned by mail; have the return made to a fictitious address. Your real title will eventually be lost, but perfectly acceptable quasi-counterfeit titles and registration documents can be made using an old title and registration as models on the computer (quasi-counterfeit documents are perfect reproductions of real documents that exist somewhere). Have these blank documents in hand before leaving town.

Drop your old car off in a large shopping center, where it will be impossible to determine who dropped it off or when, and where discovery could take weeks or months. Assuming the authorities are hot for your body and that intense investigation will follow, cross the border into Mexico or Canada within eight hours of departure. Plan to hang out across the border for at least 30 to 45 days.

At most, you will need a current car registration and perhaps a driver's license to enter either place by car. Canadians seldom ask vehicle owners for ID, and Mexicans can always be bribed to "hurry up." Arrival by commercial carrier will always require more documentation because the carrier's agents do some investigation for the authorities in whose country they operate. Yet numerous visitors have faked ID to get into either country.

Once safely ensconced in Mexico or Canada, concentrate on three things: keeping a low profile, living as cheaply as possible, and setting up your computer system (if you were able to bring it with you) to reproduce helpful documents. Keep away from the United States as long as finances and patience will allow.

Canada doesn't require anything, but you will need a new birth certificate and/or driver's license to reenter the States. Theoretically, you have had six to eight weeks in which to select and prequalify potential medium-to-large cities in which to establish a new ID. Your new location should be conveniently across the state line from a medium-to-large city. Should either city be a university city or, for some other reason, consist of a large transient population, this is a plus.

## MANUFACTURE NEW ID
## DOCUMENTS ON COMPUTER

Set the computer up again or go out and purchase a new system if you were unable to bring yours along. Start producing business cards, tax documents, union cards, letterhead, and other important privacy documents.

Using the address of a cheap flophouse in an adjoining city, file necessary death certificate papers with the state bureau of vital statistics. Depending on your circumstances, it may be wise to wait several months to file and to travel several hundred miles to another city in which to "officially die." Unless your case is extremely high profile, notify your former local paper to run a death announcement.

Using a remanufactured birth certificate, obtain a new Social Security card. If you are not a glib talker, do this by mail on the basis of being under the age of 16. If you are a good actor, go to the Social Security office in person to get your number after having "spent 40 years in a religious society."

From this point, you can expand into all sorts of real ID, such as driver's license and, in some circumstances, a new passport. After you become proficient with your computer system, it is amazing how many real documents are easily made up at home and how you can get along without many real documents.

### ESTABLISH YOUR NEW CAREER

While all of this is going on, be sure not to neglect the business aspect of your new life. Remember that you cannot go on welfare and avoid being tracked by giant computers.

Set up your new company (in a different line of work than you previously were in), open a bank account, and begin to work in the underground economy. Be certain not to engage in any overtly illegal activities, especially those having to do with drugs, robbery, or guns, and be especially careful not to commit any traffic violations. During this time, it is also wise to work vigorously on remaking your appearance, mannerisms, vocation, and habits. You may have a phone installed in your new name, but *never* use it to contact old friends and relatives. State, federal, and private investigators will be all over these people's phone records like a bad smell. One wrong call on your part will blow the most elaborate cover.

## HAVE AN ESCAPE PLAN IF THINGS GO WRONG

If plausible, nonparanoid, real evidence surfaces that the authorities are getting close, fold your tent and get out immediately. Produce a new set of documents and start all over, perhaps even killing off the old you again. Usually the tip-off that someone is looking is a landlord, neighbor, or employer mentioning that someone called or that some men were around asking about a missing person that resembles your old self.

## CUT ALL TIES WITH YOUR PAST

Remember that you can be traced by having any links with your previous employment, friends and relatives, personal traits and characteristics, hobbies, church, or records. Even the need for medication can be used to find some otherwise well-hidden new IDers. Think long and hard before doing any activity that can, under any circumstances, be turned around and used to trace you to your present location. One single mother who snatched her two small children five years ago and who spent thousands of dollars moving from state to state was easily discovered solely because her new mailing address listed three correct matching first names. The computers did all the work.

After eight or ten months in a new location, many new IDers become comfortable and confident regarding their new identity because, under normal circumstances, they will not have to show any ID. Unfortunately for the average new IDer, local and national police always assume few if any humans can make so complete a break. Unfortunately, the authorities are often correct.

# CONCLUSION

At present, many people of a freedom-loving persuasion believe that the computer era is in the process of ushering in worldwide freedom on an unprecedented level. They believe that knowledge is power and that current levels of personal knowledge can do nothing but increase. Knowledge derived from computers, they gloat, can never again be contained or controlled by any central authority.

There is a certain validity to their observation that knowledge is power and that this power can sometimes lead to freedom. And it has also been observed that, in spite of mighty efforts on the part of some governments, technology cannot be "disinvented." So when freedom advocates claim that government will never "bell that cat," they are on strong historical ground.

Yet anyone who has looked out at the real world in which we live must conclude that it isn't that simple. Governments have a tremendous ability to co-opt technology for their own use. A hundred years ago, it was commonly said that universal telephones would make us all free. Not known at that time was the government's ability (and desire) to tap telephones in large numbers. Today there are even computer "nursemaids" that sit silently, waiting to be triggered by key words such as *guns*, *bombs*, or *attack*.

Although home production of excellent, virtually detection-proof ID documents has become technologically feasible, the government has become very adept at taking the same computer-driven system to create huge, previously unheard of data banks on most citizens. As recently as 1975, no one would have supposed, for instance, that data banks for vehicle owners, welfare recipients, Social Security cardholders, and criminals of record would have been brought together under one giant web.

Several firms now sell CDs containing millions of names, complete with large data files on each name, to skip tracers. These files are upgraded monthly with everyone who takes out a postal box, licenses a car, or acquires a driver's license, and these firms aren't even government entities!

There are those who argue that government is so slow and inefficient and that the computer industry is changing so rapidly that we should not be concerned. Government, by its very nature, can never catch up, one fellow argued recently.

Nevertheless, my experience as a private investigator has shown me that it is no longer possible to hide anyplace in the world. As I have frequently boasted, pay the money and I will always find you, wherever you are—even in northern China. It has been close at times, but so far no one has proved me wrong.

The problem for investigators and others in pursuit of missing people is twofold: (1) In private industry it involves paying the bill—locating a snatched kid in London can easily run between $10,000 and $15,000; (2) in the case of government, where one might assume more skip-tracing firepower, bureaucratic bungling often intervenes, with the net result that governments often don't find people as well or as quickly as you would initially suppose.

Twenty years ago, locating another deceased person's birth certificate for personal use was a viable strategy. Many who used this plan then are still living lives free of their past today. From time to time, accounts surface of these long-lost new IDers finally returning to long-abandoned spouses. Public reaction is usually surprise that these folks could have stayed hidden so long and that they voluntarily chose to come forward at this time.

But then was then, and now is now. Today, those attempting this are likely to run into great difficulty. Increasingly, government record keepers are linking birth and death records. Local record holders now require additional identification, including notarized statements, records, and even driver's licenses.

Computer-generated ID can be produced with which to acquire the birth certificate of a child who died 30 years ago, but why go to all this work? It is easier to produce needed birth certificates at home. If that new ID wall starts to crumble, you can produce another or locate a county where all records were lost and develop your own document "originating" from the lost era. Even if you manage to successfully hide behind a new birth certificate from a dead child, other methods can be brought to bear to find you.

New IDers are finding that the best strategy is to use modern technology against the searchers who are using high-tech equipment to track them down, thereby raising the price of finding them so high that the game is never worth the candle. Computers, scanners, and printers can be used to effect this happy paradox.

The relatively new tactic of filing bogus death certificates can also be deployed, at least for a time. Imagine a client's dilemma when an investigator comes up with records showing that the client's ex-spouse died in a Nashville flophouse a year ago, but a hoax is suspected. "For another six grand I will check it out for you," the PI says. So then, the price is ratcheted up again, to hopefully unacceptable levels for the pursuer.

Never forget that those wanted by the authorities for something especially heinous often only delay their being discovered. Governments are the only entities that have unlimited budgets, and they regularly allow their minions to exceed them. But, as mentioned, mighty disincentives often preclude government authorities from taking decisive action.

Keep in mind that this volume is for basically good citizens who find that they must start over again with a new ID and who can expect to live a somewhat normal existence, somewhere, somehow.

As usual, anyone with any new ideas or suggestions can reach me through Paladin Press.